BY OLIVIA GATWOOD

Life of the Party

New American Best Friend

LIFE of the PARTY

LIFE of the PARTY

Poems

OLIVIA GATWOOD

THE DIAL PRESS

NEW YORK

Published in the United States by The Dial Press,
an imprint of Random House, a division of
Penguin Random House LLC, New York.

THE DIAL PRESS and the HOUSE colophon are
registered trademarks of Penguin Random House LLC.

Trade Paperback ISBN 978-1-9848-0190-6
Ebook ISBN 978-1-9848-0191-3

Printed in the United States of America on acid-free paper

randomhousebooks.com

9 8 7 6 5

Book design by Barbara M. Bachman

CONTENTS

PART I

PART II

PART III

AUTHOR'S NOTE

In June in Boston, the sun rises at 5:10 A.M. I know this because, one week, I stayed up every night until that exact minute. I can't quite recall what I was up doing—maybe pacing my kitchen, moving between my couch and my bed, starting movies hoping I would fall asleep and then stopping them when I didn't. I am not an insomniac. Far from it—I've never had trouble clocking ten hours of sleep when I need it. My sleepless week, and the several more all-nighters between then and now, happened because I was afraid. I was afraid of something very specific: a man climbing through my first-floor apartment window, which realistically could have been popped open with a butter knife, and strangling me in my bed.

It feels both important and irrelevant to tell you that I spent months before that week almost exclusively consuming true crime. Important because, yes, my fear was shaped by the dozens of stories I'd read and watched that mirrored my phobia, stories that showcased how common and easy it is to murder a girl. One could argue (many did) that had I not read those stories, I would not have kept all of my windows closed in the middle of the summer in an apartment without air-conditioning.

This media obsession of mine is simultaneously irrelevant

because even without it, my fear had been validated over and over by very real, very tangible experiences. There was the first time I lived alone, at eighteen, when a stranger saw me on the street, figured out my address, and left notes on my door insisting that we belonged together. There was the man who tried to pry open my roommate's window with a crowbar while she slept. The man who sat in the back of my show and laughed every time I talked about women's deaths. The man who forced open my car door in my driveway and climbed on top of me as I tried to get out. The American boys in another country who placed bets on who would sleep with me first while they walked me home, how I left them on a street corner in the middle of the night so they wouldn't know where I was staying. And there were all of the men before, between, and after that—men whose names I know, men I loved and trusted—who violated my body, the bodies of my friends, the bodies of their daughters, and, I'm certain, the bodies of countless women I do not know.

People often tell me that I spend too much time being afraid of something that is statistically less likely than a car crash. But every time I read the news, I am pummeled by stories of missing girls, murdered girls, women killed by their revenge-seeking former boyfriends, and it becomes increasingly difficult to call the murder of women "rare." It is impossible to call my fear "irrational."

I want to believe that the motivation behind most true crime is to bring to light the epidemic of women's murder worldwide, to use nonfiction storytelling as a method of illuminating a clear pattern. But I don't believe that. If that were true, it wouldn't focus on crimes committed by random strangers, and instead would reveal the much more common perpetrators: men whom these women knew and often loved. If true crime were truly mission-oriented, it would focus on the cases that are *not* explicitly perverse and shocking, the ones that are familiar, fast, and happen at home. If true crime sought to confront the reality of violence against women, it would not rely so heavily on fear-mongering narratives of cisgender white girls falling victim to men of color. Instead, it would acknowledge that indigenous women experience the highest rates of homicide, often at the hands of white men. It would depict the stories of the several transgender women murdered each month, or the countless black, brown, and indigenous women who have gone missing without so much as an investigation.

The language of true crime is coded—it tells us our degree of mourning is contingent on the victim's story. While students and athletes are often remembered for their accolades and looks, sex workers or women who struggled with addiction are reduced to those identities as a justification for the violence committed against them—if their stories are even covered at all. The truth is: It is a privilege to have your body looked for. True crime, while being a genre that so many women rely on for contorted validation, is, simultaneously, a perpetuator of misogyny, racism, and sexualized violence—all of which is centered around one, beloved, dead girl. It is a genre primarily produced by men. A genre that complicates how we bond over our love for it, often unsure of who identifies with the victim and who identifies with the perpetrator.

I found true crime because of my fear. A fear that, for so long, felt absurd and loud and wholly my own. True crime taught me that I am not the only one being devoured by this anxiety. And I am not the only one whose reaction is to consume as much true crime as possible—to fuel and fight it at once. But the true crime I want is written by women. The true crime I want moves beyond the star athlete. I want the stories that honor girls, not sensationalize them. The true crime I want knows that more than half of the women murdered worldwide are killed by their partners or family members. The true crime I want does not celebrate police or prison as a final act of justice, but recognizes these systems as perpetrators too—defective, corrupt, and complicit in the same violence that they prosecute.

As an avid consumer of true crime in all genres—short stories, documentaries, podcasts, television shows—and as a writer myself, I began to wonder what stake poetry has in that conversation. What happens when we look at the phenomenon of our obsession with homicide and we say, "This is how this makes me *feel*. This is what this does to me at night."

I want to look beyond true crime to understand why I feel the way I do. I want to look at my own life, at the lives of women I love, women I've lost, women in my community and beyond, and begin to understand that the fear inside me is a product of simply being alive.

Yes, I am terrified of being murdered. I am terrified that a man who threatened me on the Internet will come to one of my shows with a gun. I am terrified of rejecting men harshly because of the backlash that comes with it. I am not terrified because true crime told me to be, I am terrified because I have been here long enough to know I should be. This feeling dictates the ways I move: in parking garages, at bars, in my own house. And I have grown to know this feeling so intimately that I also experience a need to protect it—to understand where it was born, to name it, and to say it out loud.

This is a book of poems about true crime. It is also a book of poems about the many small violences a person can withstand. It is a book about memory and girlhood. This book is, in large part, a memoir of my fear and how it was planted in me as a child, then perpetuated throughout my adult life. This book remembers the ways I have watched women I love disintegrate at the hands of men they trusted, girls found and not found, and, ultimately, how I have healed while keeping some necessary part of this fear intact. Reader, I cannot promise you will be less afraid when you finish this book, but I hope you will feel more able to name what lives inside you.

I asked earlier what stake poetry has in this conversation. The only answer I have is this: to help us feel less alone in the dark.

I.

Sometimes the girls who walk alone
Aren't found for days or weeks

—TRACY CHAPMAN

GIRL

after Ada Limón

i don't think i'll ever not be one
even when the dozen grays sprouting
from my temple take hold and spread
like a sterling fungus across my scalp,
even when the skin on my hands is loose
as a duvet, draped across my knuckles,
even when i know everything there is to know
about heartbreak or envy or the mortality
of my parents, i think, even then i'll want
to be called *girl,* no matter the mouth
it comes from or how they mean it,
girl, the curling smoke after a sparkler
spatters into dark, *girl,* sweet spoon of crystal sugar
at the bottom of my coffee, *girl,* whole mouth
of whipped cream at the birthday party, say *girl,*
i think, i'll never die, i'll never stop running
through sprinklers or climbing out of open windows
i'll never pass up a jar of free dum dums
i'll never stop ripping out the hangnail with my teeth
i'm a good girl, bad girl, dream girl, sad girl
girl next door sunbathing in the driveway
i wanna be them all at once, i wanna be
all the girls i've ever loved,
mean girls, shy girls, loud girls, my girls,
all of us angry on our porches,
rolled tobacco resting on our bottom lips
our bodies are the only things we own,
leave our kids with nothing when we die
we'll still be girls then, too, we'll still be pretty,
still be loved, still be soft to the touch

pink lip and powdered nose in the casket
a dozen sobbing men in stiff suits
yes, even then, we are girls
especially then, we are girls
silent and dead and still
the life of the party.

and no one is there to hear it
       here's what happens. i'll tell you.
       if she is in the woods, it shoots
       from the cannon of her throat
       & smacks itself against a branch,
       whips around it like a tetherball.
       if she is facedown in the moss,
       it seeps into the forest floor's pores,
       & every time a hiker passes through,
       the days beyond her unravel,
       & steps along the sponge-green floor,
       a small howl will fan out from beneath his feet.
       if the girl is in the city,
       the scream gets lodged
       in the cubby of a neighbor's ear,
       prevents him from sleeping at night
       & so, naturally, he sells it to a secondhand store.
       he takes it to the buying counter
       in a jewelry box & says,
       i don't know who this belonged to
       but i don't want it anymore.
       & though the pierced & dyed employee
       is reluctant to take it, she sees the purple
       bags like rotting figs under the neighbor's eyes
       so she offers store credit.
       & so as not to startle customers,
       a small label will be placed on the box
       that says A SCREAM & each time a person cracks
       it open the girl's rattling tongue will shake loose
       into the store. this happens for months but no one
       wants to buy it, to take care of it. everyone wants

to hear it once to feel something & then go back
to their quiet homes, so the store throws it
in a dumpster out back, where the garbage
truck picks it up & smashes it beneath
its hydraulic fists. the scream will get buried
in a landfill somewhere in new jersey
& later the landfill will be coated in grass,
where a wandering child will see a hill,
will throw her body against it
& shriek the whole way down.

GHOST STORY FOR MASTURBATING AT SLEEPOVERS

after Melissa Lozada-Oliva

have you heard the one about the girls
in sleeping bags littered across the living room floor,
faces next to each other's feet, bellies full on pantry food
and quiet, eyes vigilant to a black cube television?

in my version it goes like: one girl slithers out into the dark
and whispers the song of herself.
soon, they are all on their stomachs,
pushing up against long johns
with the mounds of their palms,
and no one names what is happening, both because
it will become real and because there is not a name
for it yet, only the knowledge
that whatever it is must not be said aloud.

in another version, a mother is falling into a still sleep,
certain that her daughter has not yet discovered
that what swells is not always a wound. she wakes,
hours later, to an orchestra of breath in the next room
and makes her way down the hall, hovers in the doorway,
and sees a dozen girls in white, quivering against the carpet.

for a moment, a small chaos blooms in her sternum,
cheeks erupt with blood, the dance of denial
in her stomach, and then she remembers her own
small ghosts—the curl of her best friend's toes in a room
like this one, breath echoing from her pillow
back into her mouth again and again, like this,
until she grew tired and resolved herself into the floor.

Once, everything was a gift. Once, anything
resembling the thing we wanted was the thing
we wanted. We were not yet gangly and scowling
at the generic cereal in the cabinet
or knock-off Adidas slides with four stripes.

When we begged for a swimming pool and my father
filled trash cans with hose water, we saw
what was made for our bodies and no one else's;
when he built a playhouse from splintered
plywood, with a metal slide, we saw a giant
silver tongue spilling into the dirt.

When the sun lifted itself to its highest point,
a proud bully, and the city became a third-degree
burn, we ignored the desert curfew and instead
heard the slide singing, *One more ride,*
imagined ourselves floating without burns
to the ground. So I stood at the top, naked
under my dress, and let my legs unfold in front
of me, lace parachute ballooning from my hips,
bare butt to the metal, blisters hatching
like small eggs, rising, pink yolks,

I heard the drought laughing
with its smoker's throat:
   There's no water for you here.

the pain I don't say
out loud, builds a home
inside me.

Dylan got busted for bringing a bullet to school & when he
slipped the casing out of his pocket like a rare pill we were all
certain that the hollow point would explode at any second, our
bodies tense and heavy like a dozen dying suns, we imagined
his hand blown to confetti but I knew he came from a family
that shot big game, I knew they had a meat freezer & glass-
eyed deer on every wall, so it wasn't his fault he didn't see bul-
lets the way the rest of us did, something he could toss up and
catch in his palm with ease & it was the same year my lips were
so chapped that the red crack ran up beneath my nose & I
couldn't stop licking the wound & when I left class to hold my
burning mouth against the water fountain, Frankie was passed
out & bleeding from his forehead on the hallway floor & Ms.
Rosemary said I might have saved his life, whether that's true,
I don't know, what I do know is that Frankie was a redheaded
soundless child & after that he wouldn't stop talking about al-
most dying but never gave me credit for discovering his body
& the next week Jeremy launched himself off a swing set & his
forearm bone shot through his bent wrist, I saw it, anyway, I
heard the word *fractured* in a spelling bee so when I ran to tell
Ms. Amy, I was set on flaunting my new vocabulary but the
hard corners jutted into my cheeks & my memory went soft &
so I just stood there stuttering about the skeleton & finally,
when Ms. Amy found Jeremy in the grass, the word wriggled
its way into my mouth & I shouted, *It's fractured!* & Ms. Amy
whipped & snapped, *It's so much more than that,* but I was just
happy to have spoken my new language & then there was the
family of baby pink mice in the reading corner & Carl, my fa-
vorite custodian, had to remove them, but rumor has it that he
gathered them in a sock & smashed them under a rock in the
parking lot & I couldn't look at him the same after that, based

on my understanding he was a murderer of tiny things & we were tiny things, I remember, even then, understanding the smallness of myself, of all of us & the way we had to dodge & skip through the world like rodents under the boots of men, except for once, when Miguel went on vacation to Mexico & was killed in a collapsed cave & we planted him a tree but it was just a seedling, no taller than my right knee & when we all stood in a circle to wish him goodbye, I remember looking at the struggling plant, its wiry arms & frail trunk & feeling, for the first time, big.

[my favorite pastime is watching the baby-
sitter put her hair into a ponytail. she
smooths it flat against her scalp & even
when i think it must be perfect she smooths
it again, gathers the overflow in her fist
and removes a black elastic from her wrist,
stretches and slaps till there's no slack,
splits the tail in two & yanks the arms
apart, forehead skin strained taut against
her skull, eyebrows pulled to an arch like a
doll drawn happy.]

THE FIRST SHAVE

I am nine.
We are bored
and Karen is dying.

We drove to Austin
that summer
so Sarah's dad—

who described Karen as
*the great and impossible love
of his life,* who taught us

the word *lymphoma* and then
the concept of the prefix,
how it explains where the tumor lives—

could say goodbye.

The house is a rind
spooned out by the onset of death,
what's left is a medicine cabinet

full of razors & we are hungry
& alone & sitting
on the living room floor

where the light
from a naked window
slices the hardwood

like melon, exposes
each individual fuzz
on my scabbed calf,

a field of erect, yellow poppies
& we have been alive as girls
long enough to know

to scowl at this reveal
& what better time
than now to practice removal.

Once, I watched my mother
skin a potato in six
perfect strokes.

I remember this
as Sarah teaches me
to prop up my leg
on the side of the tub

and runs the blade
along my thigh. *See?*
she says. *Isn't that so much better?*

Before we left Albuquerque
her father warned us,
She will have no hair,

a trait
we have just
begun to admire

except, of course,
for the hair he is talking about,
that which we hold against our necks,

that which will get us
husbands or compliments
or scouted in a mall,

eventually cut off
by our envious sisters
while we sleep.

tight buns at the napes of their necks
hair combed slick behind their ears
& middle parts so straight they might
have been split with a razor by their mothers
that morning. they didn't wear jewelry except
for purity rings & golden rosaries, thin chains
crawling over the humps of their clavicles.
there was no word for *godless* then
so i lied, said i too had a first communion
wore a buttercream dress & all the photos
were in storage, memorized the prayers
i needed & said them as bored as i could,
played apathetic towards my new king.
jenna believed me until she came over
& quietly scanned the walls of my parents' house,
which were empty mostly except for a few
paintings of fish & men carrying fruit.
finally, upstairs, she whispered that she knew
i wasn't a girl of the lord, that she wouldn't tell
anyone as long as i told her what i was.
i am nothing, i said, prouder than i meant it.
she was forgiving & offered to take me to church
so that i could learn how to receive the bread,
wish peace, all of the holy dances
i had never practiced. we rehearsed there,
played church in my bedroom
& she was the priest, taught me how to cup
my hands, how to place it on my tongue.
finally, i got it down pat, enough to make
it look like muscle memory & jenna seemed
regretful, then made me promise to make myself
believe in it or we'd both be sent to hell.

ADDENDUM TO NO BAPTISM

When I tell the story of the slide
at parties, or poetry readings
or wherever I might indulge
in the business of handing over a tale
as perfect as a clean and burped infant,
I leave out the ending.

Know your audience
is something I hear people say.

And so I don't say the part
where a man saw a child's
burning body and announced
his hand a healer.

And so, I end the story in my scream,
not in my silence, facedown
on a card table in the backyard
while the next-door neighbor
hovered his splayed fingers
above my newborn wound,
how he promised if I focused
hard enough, closed my eyes,
listened to my breath, I would
feel something. *Energy,* he called it.

No need for a doctor, he said,
and somehow I knew, the sooner I said
it worked, the sooner he would
stop floating above me.

So I swallowed each welt,
said, *All better,* and climbed
from atop the table,
pulled my dress back over
my knees and did my best to walk
with no limp, inside.

[i dream of knowing the babysitter in her other life. the one where she doesn't apologize for cursing & shows me where she hides whatever she hides. she gave me a jacket & in it, i found an eighth-grade school schedule, folded & soft from the washer, in the pocket. i kept it in my desk drawer, studied it at night, ran my finger over the class abbreviations, ENG 009, HIS 009, MAT 010, calculated the time gap between each class—seven minutes, *how do you get from one end of the building to the other in seven minutes?* i coiled & split from the anxiety, grieved for the safety of a single classroom, a teacher who goes by their first name— wanted to ask her so bad how she did it, how she made it out alive, but i didn't want to give myself away, instead i watch her walk around her bedroom & take notes on the way she moves—precise, everything has a correct place, seems like she's always cleaning, always putting something away— she's fast & i wonder how she became that. maybe she always has been, maybe she never had to learn how.]

ADDENDUM II TO NO BAPTISM

I should also mention that I don't know
if his hands ever touched me, though they did.

This distorted fact might also be a reason
I leave out the ending. Another rule
to good storytelling is that no one wants
a half-remembered tragedy. You must
know the width of the knife and how
it ruined you, name the organs it kissed.

Maybe he touched me, maybe again,
maybe that is why for years I wrapped my mouth
around anything that would fill it
is not beautiful. It is a bouquet
of the bitter and half-bloomed.

Sometimes, the writer in me
wants to remember just so I can give
you a story. Sometimes, I think
the memory will appear in my doorway,
first a shadow, then a man, stepping
into the light.

memory, too,
lives in my body
not my brain.

some girls were seasoned in sex,
visibly bored when the conversation
lingered around foreplay but never
nosedived beyond it. some girls
had done it, but with their boyfriends
who were still boys & still loved them,
which made it not count.

it didn't matter if you were a virgin
or not, it mattered how you used it,
like currency, a sack of nickels
on the bar top. it was before any of us
believed we were good at anything,
so we became good at our bodies,
at talking about them like we were
greyhound bitches, lean & itching
to break through the race gates.

before either of us had sex,
jordan & i showed up to the skate park
in plaid skirts with no panties
& the boys took turns sticking
their faces underneath, like small
children lining up behind a telescope,
giddy for a suddenly reachable universe.

jordan brought a disposable camera
& the boys snapped photos
of their skirt-submerged
heads, us with our hands
over our mouths like amateur
marilyns, knock-kneed & flustered.

who knows what we got from it,
maybe a loosie or a ride or the chance
to finish a sentence & then took
the camera to the pharmacy on 4th street,
where the middle-aged woman
printed each glossy still & we paid
in quarters & she didn't ask any questions

& we hovered over them, our chests hot and skittish,
laying the best ones out like tarot cards promising
a good future. but soon we grew bored of our own faces,
grew out of our old bodies & threw the photos away

where my father found them later that week
& left them on the kitchen table for me to find.
they looked foreign against my mother's tablecloth,
a girl not welcome in this house.

he pondered over them like a poker deck,
selected one of me & a headless boy,
let it dangle between his thumb & forefinger,
waited a moment for me to drink it in,
to look myself in the eye,
& said, *who are you?*

MY MOTHER SAYS I WASN'T A BAD GIRL, I WAS JUST BORED

after Kim Addonizio

i wasn't the real thing, the bad girl by instinct
who wouldn't even call herself bad because
that would mean at one point she considered what
it might look like to be good. i was something
less lovable—woke up before the bad girl sleeping
next to me & tinkered with her makeup till noon,
followed her out the window so i could mimic
the way she bent her legs, monkey-fucked every
cigarette so i didn't get caught fumbling with
the flint wheel on some dude's bic. i swung the bat
in the right direction, undid enough belts
to fill a résumé right, but i never hailed the ride
on my own, never instigated the fight, never promised
a man i was good & meant it. the bad girl calls
her body what it is—the shit—i called my body
unfamiliar until it was looked at & then channeled
everything i'd learned from the bad girl,
how to arch the back, curl the toes, *don't be ashamed
of the veins in your neck,* she said once, *they mean
you're feeling something.* the bad girl wants everyone
around her to feel something & she wants to see proof.
once, we smoked pcp from a dr pepper can
& lay in the dark, talking about our stomachs.
she was frustrated that she couldn't see anything,
so she had me hold a lighter above my torso
while she pulled up my shirt & watched as my belly
rose & fell, each time i breathed her in.

We wasted whole days on the 66 bus,
cruising Lomas for thirty-five cents
just to remind ourselves, and whoever else
decided to look, that we were capable of transience.
But mostly, it was for the air-conditioning.

Jordan wore long sleeves that summer
and told the seventh-grade counselor
that she had *fallen into a bucket of knives,*
which, I remember thinking, was not untrue,
based on the use of the verb *fall* in other phrases,
to imply it was not particularly accidental
but more so situational, like how one might
fall in love or *fall in with a group of bad girls.*

The bus wagged and groaned from my house
to the park in about thirty minutes, at which point
we might decide to disembark, depending on how likely
it was that the boys, our only incentive, had flocked to
the usual spot beneath the overpass.

And then there was the small twitch in my belly
when we saw the circle of shaggy heads
in the distance, a pile of bikes and skateboards
next to them like a metal bonfire, or the cloud of sweet
grape smoke that met us before
they noticed we had arrived.

It often seemed at first like they didn't want us
there—an observation I had never voiced to Jordan
for fear it would make it real—but she was always

good at bartering for her presence; as soon as she spoke
you would forget what it was like to live without her.

Before the boys could decide to do something
that didn't include us, Jordan would make light of exactly
what it was we had that they didn't, usually in the form
of a complaint like, "I just want to take off my bra already,
can you help me?" And because I was *With Her,*
a title I would have preferred over my own name,
they would assume me next in line to be stripped,
as though whatever pain Jordan felt, I felt.

It wasn't long before we were in the center
of the circle playing with each other's hair
while they watched, flaunting the way we could share
our bodies where they weren't allowed. It was a gift—
to know a boy's desire and catch it in a jar,
to watch it bash its body against the glass.

If I could freeze the moment here, I would—
head on Jordan's thigh, emptying a peach
Prime Time into my throat. But of course the
debt billowed towards us with its jaw unhinged
and we were asked to walk how we speak,
to name the city we had built in the boys' bodies.

Jordan knew I was a nervous girl. Maybe that's why
she kept me around, I made her look wise,
a broken wristwatch on the forearm of her life.
And I remember when she saw me tremble,
held my cheek, smiled weakly, said,

I've got this, as though she knew all along
she would have to tame the circus by herself.

I kept lookout while she took the oldest one
behind the bushes and did whatever she did best,
which, from what I understood, was the ability
to take and take and take.

Jordan's choke becomes a groan becomes
a laugh and I breathe for the first time.
She emerges from the tall grass, water welled
in her bottom lids and smiling, like a teary-eyed mother
at a dance recital. He says something about *talent, stamina,*
ahead of her time, and she calls him a liar and he grabs her ass
with a newfound sense of purpose
and walks us to the bus stop
with an arm draped over the back of her neck while I float
a few feet away, and when he climbs on his bike to leave,
Jordan yanks him by the shirt and demands two cigarettes.

One for now to get out the taste
and one for later when I remember what I did.

By now, the sky has cracked into a shrill blue—
a final shriek before the sun plummets behind the volcanoes.
It is July, just past evening rush hour
and the city is a dying flame,
the gap of silence between hissing cars
growing longer and longer
and longer with each tender minute.

I MUST HAVE ONLY LOVED HER IN THE SUMMER

Because what I remember are her legs,
bare and speckled red from the heat,
the sour of her armpits while she talked
with her hands, or how she slept on a towel
in the gravel backyard, sun glaring
off the oil on her shoulders, or how she flipped
through her mother's catalogues, drawing genitals
stuffed into a model's mouth, or how we only wore
spaghetti straps, even at night, her finger swirling
the perimeter of a blood moon while we lay on the roof
of a car parked on the mesa, a dozen girls'
bones buried beneath
our slow-breathing bodies, years before they were discovered,
or how we took naked ice baths and swapped
sucks on a rocket pop
that we bought with loose change and how, by any definition
of what it means to be in love, we were that, but somehow
only in June, or July, or August, come September
she was gone, hibernating, waiting for the sun, her skin,
her tongue lapping up the salt on my cheek,
we only ever talked about our bodies and what we wanted
to teach them, if we couldn't tangle our legs together
we had nothing to talk about, if we couldn't dangle ourselves
in front of each other, what was the point of hanging out,
if we couldn't suck a bloody bruise into each other's necks
to make some boy jealous, who were we really?
What else was there to do?

the boys and i are playing quarters with double shots of
vodka and i am winning. by *winning* i mean i am not one
of the boys but i am the next best thing. by *the next best*
thing i mean i am a girl and i am drunk. every time i miss a
shot, johnny gets to flick a quarter against my knuckles
and now my knuckles are bleeding onto my thighs but
every time i make a shot i get to knock back a throat-full
of liquor. i slam down the glass until it cracks up the side
and now the game is about who will still drink from it,
who will risk shards in the belly, who will cut up their
insides for a pack of newports, and it's not that i even want
the cigarettes, it's just that i am not afraid of blood, which
is also part of being a girl. but being the only girl means
making yourself lose when you've won too much so i
bounce the coin off the rim of the shot glass and let
johnny slice me open. in thirty minutes, johnny is
dragging me out of the bathroom by my wrists and i can
hear him saying something about blood on the carpet,
about a drunk girl in the house who is staining everything
and i think that means i must be the champion of quarters.
johnny is the kind of guy who sleeps with a gun, not
women. but johnny is always the one inviting me over for
a game of quarters and sometimes i wonder if this is how
johnny fucks. like maybe he is the kind of man who only
screams when he is underwater or lets me feel how strong
his fingers are without actually touching me. maybe that's
why we're all here, even the boys, to let johnny hold us
like a barred window. i work a double one day a week and
on this day, don't answer johnny's call. by *one day a week* i
mean two men break in and shoot johnny in the temple
for two thousand pills and i am scraping pasta from a
businessman's plate into the trash. at some point i'll tell

you why i didn't go to the wake. i guess i never really
knew johnny like that. by *that* i mean sober or in a church.
when i say *i didn't go to the wake* i mean i drove by his house
every day for two years and the FOR SALE sign never got
taken down, like the house would always be johnny's, like
maybe the whole town knew what happened there. like
maybe no one could get rid of the blood.

THE AUTOCROSS

The men at the autocross say I could be useful
in a garage because I have tiny hands. I can reach
the deepest corners of an engine like a housemaid,
make it all brand new.

They say I'm different from other girls,
the ones splayed out across the hood
like a brand-new paint job. The ones who like the taste
of old oil under a fingernail, how easy it is
to zip off a navy jumpsuit.

The men at the autocross don't believe I know
the difference between a four-cylinder and a V6 engine
but they keep me around anyway because
I don't take up much space. They aren't bad guys.
They don't know my name, never asked,
just call me Girl Driver, which is what I am.
The men aren't wrong.

When I clock in a tenth of a second faster than Mike
in the '99 Miata, the men say it's because I don't weigh shit.
They don't know my name but they call me Cheater.
The men retighten my bolts *just for safe measure*.
The men open my car door, *Ladies first*.
The men are always helping.

One man asks how I reach the pedals.
One man asks where my daddy is.
One man opens his trunk and says,
Bet you're small enough to fit.

[the babysitter's best friend was her dog, who she trained to jump like a show pony over stacked boxes in the street. once, i saw her father on the front porch, tending to a bite wound on his calf. for weeks he swore that if her mother didn't agree to euthanize it, he would shoot it in the mouth himself.]

MURDER OF A LITTLE BEAUTY

with lines from People *magazine's 1997 coverage
of the JonBenét Ramsey murder*

Little Miss Christmas dead in the basement
ripples of shock quickly spread through the nation

rope & a blanket found near the victim
the blood & flesh of Miss West Virginia

the perfect mother, the perfect brother
a private jet for the perfect father

duct tape, a cord twisted round her neck
a prime-time interview on CNN

flirtatious, provocative, six-year-old kid
America's Royale Miss in 1996

elegant, lavish, gets all the attention
a ransom note as much as John's pension

dab your eye, we know you like it gory
only the blondes get a cover story

girls go missing right around the corner
but she needs a tiara for us to mourn her

naturally attractive, exceptionally bright
how many ways can we say the word *white*?

[i knew her father as well as a child knows a man not of her blood. i knew he stayed up late to draw blueprints of houses we would never see. let us run our fingers along their perfect lines. once, i told him a joke about blondes getting hit by trains, & he laughed so hard he fell off a playground swing into the dirt.]

WE ALL GOT BURNT THAT SUMMER

The music died that night in Albuquerque.
                              —ATMOSPHERE, *That Night*

A boy has just pressed
his mouth against me,
in a fast-food restaurant bathroom.

I think he would love me
if he let himself, if he could get past
our age difference, I say.

I am talking about my favorite musician,
a rapper twice my age, with acne scars
and black hair, a weathered face I want to know.

He tells me the last time Atmosphere
came here was a year before,
when I was still a child,
when I was young enough to believe
every year was urgent and couldn't imagine
being alive when my ID expired.

The boy tells me he was there at the concert,
his breath smells like the small fist
I had unfurled into his throat.
I like that my body is his breath now,
that I know who I am while he talks.

He'll never come back, the boy says,
because a girl was murdered the night
of the show by a custodian and went
undiscovered behind a vending machine

for four days. Everything is tragic.
Everything has either already happened
or never will.

The boy keeps saying it could have been me,
as if that concert, that night, was my only shot
at dead-girl stardom and now that I've just barely
missed the grip of some quiet janitor,
I've got a long life ahead, no hogtied future
waiting for me at the end of an alley.

But the truth is I don't feel relief.
I don't feel safe.

I am mad at her for dying.
I want him to come back,
I want him to find me.

I want to know
what it means to survive
something.

does it just mean
I get to keep my body?

the only person who knows,
and i mean *really* knows—
from even eight states away,
a pitch so gentle only
he can hear it—my sadness,
is my father who, when i was sixteen
and experiencing my first heartbreak,
knew nothing but also
knew everything at once,
and without asking any questions,
took me on the back of his
motorcycle and drove us
up to the mountains where,
in the middle of summer,
we rode the ski lift
up and down, admiring, silently,
the tall grass and blond poppies
and untouched globes of dandelion
florets and the lonely boy
at his summer job who pulled
the lever just for us, the only
customers, to lift our bodies
up this silent beast, and i
was too young to point
and say, *how beautiful,*
still stuck in my teen religion
of black eyeliner, eyes rolling,
but knew, despite my denial,
that something here was
worthy of praise and i guess
that was the lesson,

my father, who knows,
and i mean *really* knows,
my sadness, knew that i
didn't need to be told,
i needed to see, that despite
it all, there was still
something alive beneath me.

what i am trying to say is actually very simple:
my first love is dead & nothing about my life
has changed. but of course, everything is different.

of course, there is the pang of grief when i notice him,
still alive, in my older poems—once, i named him
the small boy, another time *the boy who loved me*—

& of course, there is the fact that the fear of running
into him in a shopping mall or post office
is now entirely fantastical, a dream, a relief,

the mundane becoming impossible. & of course,
i used to laugh every time "let's get it on" by marvin gaye
was playing & i would lean over to the person next to me,

no matter who it was, & i would say
i lost my virginity to this song, can you believe that?
& for a moment the person & i would sing along
together, swim in the high notes, & then i would tell

them the story about the day andrew & i
decided to have sex & how we were children,
but we were both children, which made it okay,

& we planned every detail, down to what we wore
that day. i will tell the listener i wore a skirt
because i saw it in the movies & didn't want him

to see me naked & again, what children we were,
uncovering the wet myth of sex & sometimes,
depending on who the listener is, they will stiffen

at the thought of kids & sex & i will assure them over
& over that we loved each other, *we did,* i will say,
i used up a whole disposable camera taking photos

of him & when i got them developed at the pharmacy,
i also bought a single frame & chose the picture i loved
most & propped it up next to my bed, i will say.

isn't that the most teenager thing? & the listener will relax,
comfortable now with this familiar love that they too lived
once & of course, since he died, i have not heard the song,

which means i haven't had the chance to revise
this conversation i have grown to know so well,
i imagine, perhaps, it will be exactly the same

except for the very end, when the listener begins to sink
into their chair with ease & before they reimburse me with
the story of their first love, i will say, *he's dead now,*

& something, i don't know what, will change,
the new knowledge that this small boy, this boy
who loved me, this boy who, in a small way

they love now too, is not alive somewhere.
he does not reminisce. & they will apologize
& i will tell them *it's okay.* and it is. i did not lose

someone i love. i lost someone i once loved.
i did not have to sell his furniture or start grocery shopping
for just myself. there is no phone number i call

until the new owner answers, i do not see his shoes
at my front door. he had been big for a long time.
he had not loved me for a long time.

had he called my name in the post office
or shopping mall, his voice, deep and round,
no longer in the pitchy flux of adolescence,

the song i remember—had he called my name,
before turning around,
i would not have known it was him.

[under her bed, the babysitter had miniature eques-
trian stables, a whole, tiny world beneath her sleep-
ing head—hay barrels, grooming stations, saddles, &
a racetrack. a dozen plastic horses. the babysitter
knew them all by breed: thoroughbred, arabian, ap-
paloosa, mustang. and she knew them all by the
names she'd given them herself—horse names—
boundless & sensual. i spent so long lying on my belly
on her carpeted floor, peering into the pint-sized uni-
verse that i couldn't afford, even in its diminutive
state, that i forgot the babysitter rode real horses in
real life, wore tight tan pants with knee-high leather
boots, guided the gallop through the dirt & won the
cerulean ribbons that lined her walls. once, we went
to see her ride at the state fair. no one in my family
could find her amongst the twenty-five identical girls
in helmets, perched atop the beasts' backs but i knew.
i could tell by the way she pressed against the stirrups
& stood up just slightly off the saddle, bent knees,
head forward; she was perfect. the other girls were
timid. the other girls may as well have been riding the
aluminum ponies on a carousel. the babysitter spoke
in stallion tongue, whispered in its twitching ear, *go
faster, faster, faster, now jump.*]

what I mean is that when my grandmother
called to ask why I didn't respond to her letter,
all I heard was, *Why didn't you*
text me back? Why don't you love me?

And how can I talk about my grandmother
without also mentioning that if everyone
is a teen girl, then so are the birds, their soaring
cliques, their squawking throats,
and the sea, of course, the sea,
its moody push and pull, the way we drill
into it, fill it with our trash, take and take
and take from it and still it holds us
each time we walk into it.

What is more *teen girl* than not being
loved but wanting it so badly
that you accept the smallest crumb and call
yourself full; what is more teen girl than
my father's favorite wrench, its eternal loyalty
and willingness to loosen the most stubborn of bolts;
what is more teen girl than my mother's chewed
nail beds, than the whine of the floorboards in her house?

What is more teen girl than my dog, Jack,
whose bark is shrill and unnecessary,
who has never once stopped a burglar
or heeled on command but sometimes
when I laugh, his tail wags
so hard it thumps against the wall, sometimes
it sounds like a heartbeat, sometimes I yell at him
for talking too much, for his messy room,

sometimes I put him in pink, striped polos
and I think he feels pretty,
I think he likes to feel pretty,
I think Jack is a teen girl

and the mountains, oh, the mountains,
what teen girls they are, those colossal show-offs,
and the moon, glittering and distant
and dictating all of our emotions.

My lover's tender but heavy breath while she sleeps
is a teen girl, how it holds me and keeps
me awake all at once, how sometimes I wish
to silence it, until she turns her body and
the room goes quiet and suddenly I want it back.

Imagine the teen girls gone from our world
and how quickly we would beg for their return,
how grateful would we be then for their loud enthusiasm
and ability to make a crop top out of anything.

Even the men who laugh their condescending laughs
when a teen girl faints at the sight of her
favorite pop star, even those men are teen girls,
the way they want so badly to be big
and important and worshipped by someone.

Pluto, teen girl, and her rejection
from the popular universe,
and my father, a teen girl, who insists he doesn't
believe in horoscopes but wants me to tell
him about the best traits of a Scorpio,

I tell him, *We are all just teen girls,*
and my father, having raised me, recounts the time he found
the box of love notes and condom wrappers I hid
in my closet, all of the bloody sheets, the missing socks,
the radio blaring over my pitchy sobs,
the time I was certain I would die of heartbreak

and in a moment was in love with a small, new boy,
and of course there are the teen girls,
the real teen girls, huddled on the subway
after school, limbs draped over each other's shoulders
bones knocking, an awkward wind chime

and all of the commuters, who plug in their headphones
to mute the giggle, silence the gaggle and squeak,
not knowing where they learned to do this,
to roll their eyes and turn up the music,
not knowing where they learned this palpable rage,
not knowing the teen girls are our most distinguished
professors, who teach us to bury the burst

until we close our bedroom doors,
and then cry with blood in the neck,
foot through the door, face in the pillow,
the teen girls who teach us to scream.

i never knew anything about him
except for what i saw—
not his last name
or where he'd gone to school—
just that he was a man
with a legal ID
& facial hair, a man who spoke
often about my age
as if it were a personality,
dedicated a song to me called *fifteen*
& played it while he drove me home,
dropped me off at the next block
to avoid my father, posed as a painter once,
though he was a painter,
but to get into my bedroom,
i've hired him to do a mural, i told my parents,
& my mother insisted we leave the door open
to air out the fumes, but we didn't.
instead, we fucked on the plastic sheet
& got dizzy, never finished the wall,
for years, an outline of my name
in mediocre graffiti—i think he went on to have a child
with a woman his age, i think he wrote me once
about some band that made him think of me
& i asked his daughter's name,
but before that, i know someone
must have warned me
& i must have defended it
the way a teen girl would, some flaring
loyalty to her ageless wit,
& besides that, he had
an apartment & called me his baby.

i liked standing in the kitchen
while he watched me from the living room,
i liked waking up before him & walking
to get sandwiches, i liked to make sure
he was fed. yes, these are all moments
i remember but also moments
i am watching from the outside in,
peering through cracked blinds
in the hallway of an apartment complex
into a room with no furniture
where a girl lies on her back,
a man sitting next to her,
watching her as if he is trying to predict
the ways she will grow into herself—
if her stomach & skin will get tired,
if he will leave her when it does—
& she is saying something i can't
make out, something i can only
imagine, maybe about the future,
how she can't wait until she's old
enough to move out & come here,
how she thinks the sink is the perfect
size to give their baby a bath.

MANGO SEASON

It is mango season, and Jenna is straddling a branch,
plucking the wet, yellow muscle from the sprig.
If it's timed right, it shouldn't take more than a two-finger
tug to release them from their stems, and we always time
it right—check back every day after school until the tree
is freckled with a perfect gold—one of us, whoever's blisters
have healed to callus, will scale the trunk and do the tossing,
while the other takes the task
of catching each one before
they hit purple against the ground.

Today, I am at the base, waiting for Jenna to shout
You ready? and toss sun after sun from its sky. I have
a near-flawless track record—almost never have I let one slip
through my hands—I pile them up next to a protruding root
until all that's left are green leaves, and this is where
I wish the story ended, our bellies bare, shirts pulled
up to our chests, cradling our lumpy harvest,
as we flaunt our way back home.

You might ask why we need seventeen ripe Julie mangoes
between the two of us—rawboned girls with kneecaps
that could slice fruit—we don't. We just want to win
at the boys' game, the boys who swarm like coyotes,
who play football barefoot atop thorns, who break
each other's noses and ribs and windows, who will break
ours if we pick their blooming trees bare, but we don't care,
we get out of school before them and will collect the fruit
before them and will dig our teeth into the flesh of it
before them, bury the seeds so there's no proof
that we did it except the sticky pulp around our lips.

We aren't afraid, but we are. Jenna says they see us
as kids now, but the beatdowns will be different when
they don't. There is a special hatred reserved for women
and women alone. She says her brother warned her
that something is changing. *They talk about your legs,*
he said, a nick in the glass before the crack begins to spread.

Today, before Jenna can make the leap and meet me
on the ground, the boys are home early and hungry—
find us yellow-handed and don't take so much
as a minute to say *thief* before their nails are buried
in my biceps, and Jenna can't save me, can't use her
brother's name to spare me this time because he is here,
his button-down split just a little lower than normal,
as if to coax a chest hair with the sun, and silent.

Jenna has never told me the wrong thing to do.
She told me which trees are a home for fire ants,
Don't climb them, which pads will make me stink,
Don't use them, which girls will cut my hair in my sleep,
Don't love them, and she was right, every time.
Today she yells, *Just do what they say,* while I'm dragged
from view and she stays trapped as the rest
of the boys pace beneath her feet.

They take me to an abandoned police station.
The one near the dumpster where I once found a litter
of puppies and when I got caught feeding them,
a neighbor lady put them in a garbage bag and threw
them in the back of a dump truck. Back here,

the grass is forgotten, slick and cold against your thighs.
Back here, everything and everyone is forgotten
except me. I am the star of the show. I am sitting
in an interrogation room while they decide what to do
with this harvest they pulled in the form of a girl.

One notices a shower in the corner, a burgundy
drain like rusting teeth and stained tile,
and points me towards it.
They take turns stepping inside—first a boy, then his tongue,
then a boy and then his tongue—and yes, I said no—
yes, I laughed to soften the blow, until the last one,
the one whose fingers brought me here, brings forth
Jenna's brother, half-hatched boy who I knew
so well, but now looks like a waning moon,
and demands he press his face hard against mine.

When I found the puppies, Jenna's brother
wanted to hold them, but wasn't sure how. He squatted
down next to me in the dirt and watched as I took each
newborn into my arms. He seemed nervous, like he didn't
trust his own ability to be soft.
So I took the infant and placed it
in his cupped hands, taught him to run his thumb from
forehead to snout, to rub its belly, to place it
back down in the soil
with the rest of the litter when it started to squeal. When
a younger boy wanted to try, and reached
for the dogs with a fast
and heavy hand, Jenna's brother smacked him away.
Let her teach you, he said. *Let her teach you first.*

II.

I thought how unpleasant it is to be locked out;
and I thought how it is worse, perhaps, to be locked in.

—VIRGINIA WOOLF

MY GRANDMOTHER ASKS WHY
I DON'T TRUST MEN

If you have a son, how will you love him?
She is pacing the living room,
while the Thanksgiving Day Parade
plays behind her, a montage of inflated
cartoon bodies, floating slow
down 6th Avenue, smiles
painted onto their faces.

I consider not responding.
I consider explaining that I can love him
and not trust him. I consider saying that I won't
love him at all. Just to scare her. Instead, I say,

If I am ever murdered, like,
body found in a ditch, mouth
stuffed with dirt, stocking
around my neck, identified
by my toenails, please don't go
looking for a guilty woman.

When my father and I go for a jog
on the arroyo and he runs ahead, leaving me
alone with my breath and an empty trail,
I keep running—but now, from something.
When I cross a coyote drinking from the ditch,
I am relieved it is an animal. When I see him,
my father, stretching against a tree, I scream
at him for leaving me alone. He grabs my shoulders
as if to shake my loose parts into place.

What are you afraid of? he asks. *Why are you so afraid?*

I don't know why I'm doing this—
playing show and tell with the times I've walked fast
in the dark. Maybe I see myself in the worst of it.
Maybe if I can imagine myself in the shallow
water, you should too. Maybe I am tired
of hearing people talk about the murder
of girls like it is both beautiful
and out of the ordinary.

I ask the hotel attendant
to put me in a room near the elevator.
I listen to my best friend breathe
on the line while she walks home.
Sometimes I search "woman's body found in"
when I visit a new city. Then, I learn her name.
Her age. Where they found her—under a baseboard,
limbs folded into a closet. I learn her hobbies—
that she loved to sing. I watch the security footage
they discovered of her last moments, I watch her move
and breathe like the rest of us. I watch her look
over her shoulder three times
before walking out of view.

I know my fear better
than I know
my own body.

After fingering me in a dorm room at a school neither of
us attends, the boy says he loves him—the man who
resembles my father, wearing a butter-yellow sweater,
awaiting the electric chair, hot-shot scholar in the business
of burying girls. But when he says it, the boy doesn't add
that he also likes craft beer, he isn't on a podcast or
at a party, he isn't explaining *necrophilia* to a room of girls,
he is whispering—he lets it creak up the doorstep of my
neck and sits up, hides his face, hunches at the edge of
the bed with his back towards me. He whimpers,
chants a prayer to his naked thighs—*Maybe it's in me,
maybe it's in me, maybe it's in me to do it too.* The boy has a
girlfriend named Wren or Willow, who today resized
the ring he gave her three months ago and, right before
this moment, FaceTimed him to show off how the rose-
gold now hugs the neck of her skinny finger just right.
I stood on the other side of the phone, blowing cigarette
smoke into his face while he talked. But now, the boy
has lived five minutes past being inside of my body
and he is crying on a twin-sized cot, he is telling me
she won't let him choke her, *not like you do,* he is saying,
you're what I've always wanted. I place my hand on his
back and move it in a small circle, I ask him about his
childhood, if he ever thought to hurt a rodent. I am not
concerned, I just live for a good reckoning. The man at
the edge of my bed is afraid of himself, which makes me
not afraid of him. I get on my knees behind him and
lean my chest against his back. I put my mouth at his
sideburns and let my warm breath spill onto his cheek.
I love him too, I say, *I think about him all the time.*

[by the time i was old enough to no longer
be watched but young enough to be left
out of conversations, the babysitter was
doing heroin. i know because i heard. an-
other thing i heard: there are two ways to
be found on the side of the road. dead or
almost dead. the babysitter was found the
second way.]

Liam drowned the summer before in the same lake, and it was the first time I was handed the responsibility of death like a heavy and wailing newborn. Most times, when we name tragedy like this, as a plot point, it is to center the dead in ourselves, illuminate their legacy and demise as an opportunity to teach the listener about who we have become.

And yes, that is true. But the reason I tell you about Liam's body, discovered by a fisherman, dear reader, is to help you understand the fabric of the air the first time I returned to the site of his grave. I want to note that it was not intended to be that, a revisiting, a memorial, but that the pollution of death is thick and unforgiving. I want you to understand why this story remains loud in the legend of my life, and somehow, the nature of his going makes it so.

When Eric, whose first three fingers had been cut off in his father's butcher shop, or lost in a knife fight, depending on who you ask, puts me on the black, rubber tube, pulls me by his Jet Ski in zigzags across the surface, I decide to let go before being thrown, and, like a lucky stone, or nameless pebble, depending on who you ask, I skip and tumble and come up stripped clean, clothed in bruises, treading in his wake.

When I go into the water to pee the boys swim behind me and yank me under by my hair, hold me there until I pretend to go limp. Aaron shits and, when it comes up floating, throws it into the bushes.

JoJo and I fuck in the tent and he doesn't finish, throws an empty condom into the dirt and the next morning, as we shove newspaper into the firepit, Eric finds the rubber and puts it on his own dick, dances around the growing fire, and somehow, now, everyone has been inside me.

Before leaving, the boys decide we need liquor for the road, but we have no money so Aaron suggests we pull a runner at the mini-mart and I agree to stay in the car while they go inside, and, in case you haven't caught on, I am not wearing any clothes, just a striped string bikini, because that's how they like it, and when JoJo comes sprinting back, he says Eric got locked inside the store and tosses a twelve-pack of High Life into my arms, tells me to run, and so, I do, down an alley, barefoot and damp, and it's not long before the owner of the shop, a woman in a blue Mustang, comes peeling through the dust and traps me between her headlights and a cement wall and the boys are gone and she tells me to walk to the road, while she trails behind, the hot gravel bullying my feet, and I wait on the shoulder for the police and still the boys have disappeared, a story I am not unfamiliar with here. It seems, somehow, Elephant Butte Lake has made a hobby out of taking my boys and leaving me to carry the weight.

Here is the best part.

The woman takes my photo and tells me I am banned from the town, her store, the water, even the highway that slices through, and I say,

You mean I don't have to come back?

And she says,

Never. Never let me see your face here again.

1. I told a joke to the babysitter's father & he laughed
   so hard he fell off the swing. He laughed so hard
   he asked me to come inside.

2. The first time a boy kissed me, his friends laughed,
   their torsos throbbing to the same beat, while he lodged
   his tongue inside my throat until I choked.

3. Laughter requires modification in our breathing patterns.

   EXAMPLE: WHILE I STRUGGLE TO BREATHE, SO DOES THE MAN.

4. At the bakery where I work, my boss asks me to visit
   him in his office three times a day, where he details
   the things he would like to do to my teenage body.

5. Today, a policeman sits next to him. When my boss says,
   I would fuck you against a wall, the cop laughs
   so hard he has to hold on to his duty belt.

6. The boys make it a game to throw me off the Jet Ski
   as close to the rocks as they can get without killing me.

7. The boys make it a game to leave me in the park at night
   until I think they're not coming back.

8. The boys make it a game to hold me underwater.

9. Laughter does not replace a sentence, it punctuates it.
   Where someone might pause to cough or breathe,
   laughter takes its place.

EXAMPLE: WHERE I GASP FOR AIR, THE MAN LAUGHS.

WHERE I BARTER, THE MAN LAUGHS.

WHERE I SCREAM, THE MAN LAUGHS.

10. At the house party, I am asleep in the guest room.
    I am woken up by pain. On the floor, there is a boy
    I do not know, with his hand reaching up towards
    the bed, his fingers shoved inside me, pulsing.
    He is not looking at me.
    He might as well be fumbling for his keys in the dark.

11. I leave the room wrapped in a sheet.
    The boys at the party
    love this—a panicked girl, naked under their linens.
    When I tell them, they storm the bedroom,
    pick the boy up by his arms and legs
    like a heavy net of dead mackerel,
    and toss him out onto the porch.
    They are laughing so hard
    they cannot ask me if I am okay. They cannot help me
    find my clothes.

12. The boys make it a game.

13. My boyfriend laughs
    while another man claims
    the name of the West Mesa Bone Collector.
    He tells us he can lead us to the bodies
    and my boyfriend laughs harder.

14. I am screaming behind my boyfriend's locked door.
    When I get out, his roommate sits on the sofa, laughing
    at the television, turned all the way up.

15. Years later, the roommate sees me at a bar.
    He does not say hello. Just laughs and says,
    If I had a girl who looked like you,
    I would've locked her in my room too.

16. Laughter is not about humor,
    it is about acknowledging a shared joy.
    Laughter is about bonding.

    EXAMPLE: WHEN I HEAR MEN LAUGHING,

    I DO NOT ENTER THE ROOM.

    I CRAWL HOME IN THE DARK.

And I am humming
in an ankle-length cotton dress,
hanging sheets to dry on a thin wire.
A group of girls with swollen
nipples braid each other's hair
while you watch, nod and direct
their fingers over and through,
over and through,

even the memory of their muscles
must be unlearned and retaught
by your singular truth—how to hold
a spoon or crack an egg.

We are sitting on the cusp of Spring.
We are always sitting on the cusp of Spring.

I remember what it was like
to be them—the girls—
pungent and ripe and apologizing
for every audible movement

but also looking out at the infinite tongue
of a middle-America highway and feeling joy.

I don't know what happened.

Maybe, the only reason we fall in love
is to see what we look like to someone else.

I remember when I first came here,
you told me the laundry was my duty.

You said you liked how precise I was
with cloth, praised the way I hung and folded.

I developed an affinity for bedding.

And after the night of drying,
we would unclip the sheets from the line,
lay them out on the field,
make love and fall asleep in the breeze,
all before even going inside.

We never had any clean sheets.
It was our favorite joke.

Soon, you stopped caring and I lost purpose.
I waxed and waned into a cup of bitter tea.

I have started to meditate
on all of the other things
I can do with a sheet.

How I can twist it to be rope
or drape it over my sitting body.

When you told me that you admired
the way I scrubbed a toilet, I heard,
Everything you touch becomes new.

When you told me to kill the chickens,
though I had never so much
as swatted an insect, I practiced
wringing my own ankles.

I am afraid that outside of here
is just another here. I am afraid
I will spend the rest of my life
hoping to build myself
in the vision of someone else.

What am I, if not yours?

What do I do with my hands
when they are just hands?

THE SUMMER OF 2008 AT ALTURA PARK

after Hanif Abdurraqib

The boys took me to the corner of the park
that was most hidden by trees to tell me the news.
Are you going to kill me? I joked and they
each pulled a handful of grass from the ground
and shoved it into their mouths.
I waited in silence while they looked at me
the same way my father did
when I choked on a piece of bread at dinner.

What happened was, Aaron said.
While you were away, Eric continued.
It wasn't that big of a deal, JoJo choked out
like a skipped rock across the river of his throat.

*Your boyfriend left the party with a girl
and this time, this time he came back
covered in blood, his shirt was soaked,
he threw it away, drank whiskey for the rest of the night
half-naked. When we asked what happened
he said she got a bloody nose,
said she got her period, said she was a virgin,
said she liked the pain, said sometimes you can fuck
a girl so hard you break something
no other man could reach.*

I waited for them to finish,
like I often did then with men, to stop speaking
of this girl who I imagined
must have been a blonde.

And when they sealed the confession,
I wove my fingers together in my lap
like a patient wife, knitting her own body,
pushed the girl back down to the bottom of the river,
said, *What do you mean, "this time"?*

THE LOVER AS TAPEWORM

everything
i put inside
of myself
somehow
ends up
inside
of you
instead
& so
you
grow
& i
shrink
& don't
notice
until
my best
friend
draws
me
from
the side
just by
running
a fine-tipped
pen down
a sheet of
white paper.
you walk
into a house
& swallow
all of the

furniture.
i fell
in love
with you
at parties.
when you
laughed
at my jokes,
the sound
lived
inside
of me
for weeks.
i can't tell
the
difference
between
my
thoughts
& your voice.
my intestines
& you.
how is it
possible
that you
are both
my joy
& the taker
of it?
i told you
that when
i'm sad

i do not
eat. you
said you
did not
love me
& i let
the forks
turn to rust.
you came
to the door
with
sinking
eyes &
a dry
tongue
& begged
me to
put something
inside
of myself
to make
you fat
again,
you said,
send me
a picture
of every
meal
& another
of your
clean plate.

i said,
okay
okay
okay
i will.
& so
i boiled
some
spinach
& snapped
a photo,
then
slid it
into
the dog's
bowl,
walked
to your
apartment
& left
the bare
dish
at
your
feet.

[once, the babysitter smashed her father's
hand in the hinges of her bedroom door.
when he emerged from inside their dark
& air-conditioned home, his knuckles
swathed in boxing tape, he used his good
hand to point to his teenage daughter. i
waited until bedtime to ask my parents
why. i couldn't imagine then, in my small
body, what it meant to make a rage move.
it was then i learned the word *hormones,*
my father dealt the name & repeated it
again, *teenage hormones*. i imagined it must
be a spell, the flick of a witch's wrist &
suddenly you wish your own kin bloody,
you wish his fingers gone limp.]

give me a pill
for old wounds
for the company
of parrots I lug
in my sternum
something to smother
the brag of their beaks
and then, something
to make a song
of silence, a pill
to pluck what leeches
onto my skin
before sleep
a pill to drain
the weight of water
how heavy it is
to have lived.

SOUND BITES WHILE WE PONDER DEATH

I tell my lover, as we walk through a parking garage,
    that if I ever leave
to park the car alone and don't return in five minutes,
    come looking for me.

I read that
    [runningtrailsparkinggaragessouthcarolinabedroomsvacations] are
    the [sixthfourthsecondfirstninth] most common place for women to
    be murdered
is something I tell her often to statistically justify my need
    for company in benign places.

But there are cameras, she says, pointing to the white globes
    of God's eyes
perched in every crevice, always looking in my direction.

That won't stop someone from murdering me, I say, *it'll just tell you*
    who did it.

She pauses for a moment, as if to consider the footage,
    the aerial view of my unmaking.
But maybe the fact that someone is watching will stop them.

Maybe, I say. *But I am aways stunned by the fearlessness*
    of violent men.

The garage door screams and swallows itself open.
You're such a poet, she says. And I know this is true.
I know that I am.

But mostly, I just want to be unremarkable.

THE LOVER AS CORN SYRUP

There comes a time
when you must explain
to your friends
why you stayed.

I keep writing poems
in which I compare
the lover to something
else as a way of answering
this question, so here
I am, naming the lover
as the sweetest thing
the mouth will ever know.

Here I am calling the lover
sugar's blood, the reason
behind everything I crave.

Honey, you are something
that morphs the teeth
to a murder of sitting crows,
that mothers ban from their children's
innocent lunch boxes,

something in everything
I consume, only I don't
know it until the rot creeps
in and settles in my belly,
until I am left holding my knees
on the bathroom floor,
massaging the cavity from my middle.
Until I read the back of every box.

the house is heavy with sour burning fish / when i leave / my clothes will smell / of seared salmon / sulking men on the train / will tidy their backs / twist their necks / in my direction / assume my thighs used bait / you know the thing we learn in grade school / about cheap girls' bodies / how they carry the sea / i make the train smell like gowanus / trash-river lady / all for you / you are back home writing a book / on the kitchen floor / told me this morning / you met someone else / she lives in europe / but you have more in common / like religion / your names / sound nice together / i ask for my things / you give me a garbage bag / i ask for my coat / you beg me to leave it / *it smells like you* / you say / the last time we made love / you asked me / if i was scared / i think you wanted me / to say yes / when we go to bed / all of the women scale the fire escape / perch on the rust / cackle and sing / *you can tell how much he loves her / by how he sleeps / not at all / not at all / not at all*

You plague of desert locusts born sullen in my gut,
blood-red betta eating its own tail, how I could describe
you forever as a mob, how I could learn
the name of every kind of wasp and point to you,
but I know you, my emerald heart, my wreath
of kelp, are something more timid than that—
monstrous, yes, but defenseless, also—soft
and sacred like the skin in the pit of my arm,
how I flinch and scream when my lover pokes at you,
calls you out, you, born from a mother I have not
uncovered, you, evidence of this reliable pain,
blood trickle from beneath my vest, you bigmouth
party-crasher, all talk with a plush knuckle,
you mirror made of warped wood, lying dormant
while I win, I win, I win, I win, sometimes
I dream of a surgeon, scooping you out
and stitching me back up, combing my hair
perfect over the scar, and my new smiling self
emerging, how she feels so warm, when she
hears her lover's name in another girl's mouth.

THE LOVER AS APPETITE

Gone.

ODE TO MY FAVORITE MURDER

My favorite murder
is the one that makes me sleep
in the living room, an open switchblade
resting on a coaster.

I dream of it against my neck
and move it beneath my pillow.
My favorite murder mutates

each creak into a footstep,
an echo of boots in the hallway.
This house hiccups and a man
has twelve hands, each one turning

a doorknob. No, a window.
No, he'll come in through the skylight.
I wanted to lock it last month but didn't
have a ladder. One act of laziness

becomes the loophole into my bed.
That's how it usually happens
in my favorite murders—a two-inch
plastic knob left unturned and it all fractures

into red. Of course, it wasn't the window
cracked open that caused it. We know that.
But the detail matters, somehow.
Now, I sweat the bed and fantasize
about a breeze. My favorite murder is the one
whose name I can't stop saying at parties,
whose phone call I stay awake for, whose quirks
I hoard like tennis balls in my pockets.

The movie I cast and direct.
In line at the bank, the man behind me
wears no socks with his boat shoes
and auditions for the role of killer.

In this scene, he follows me to my car.
In this scene, he watches my lover
and me have sex. He waits four nights
to kill me. When I learned that rapists

can be identified by the flesh under their victims'
fingernails, I offered to scratch my boyfriend's back.
I don't know if that method works here
because I'm not alive to see it.

I am hungry for a good story—a well-kept
diary left behind, court transcripts
and a mouthy witness. Maybe that's why
I'm writing this book.
Melissa says poetry is just obsession.

I don't know when it happened,
but one day the word *favorite*
began to mean *that which I am
most terrified of.* I have told so many men

that they are my favorite.
My favorite murders are the ones
I can place my own body into as easy
as an ad-lib, who sit on the shelf like volumes

of an almost complete encyclopedia—
all that's missing is the section on my name.

I AM ALMOST CERTAIN I COULD DISPOSE
OF MYSELF & GET AWAY WITH IT

take the burden
off his hands.
unless he loves
the regimen
i will do the burying.
clean up after
his messy project.

if a girl can be found
dead, clawing at the seams
of a walk-in freezer
or in a water tank
on the roof of a hotel
& have her death named
intentional, by her own hand,
then so can i.

i can't ask him to do it
nicely, i can't beg for no blood.
but i can make a barter
for my own removal.

i've already rehearsed
the gospel: *leave me here*
& go get a snack.
i'll touch myself
until i am my own
fingerprint. you are nowhere.
you are a man
at the park eating a banana.

i'm not trying to do him
any favors, i'm just faithful
to the way i'm found.
edwin told me once
that when the city
workers of los angeles
drained the pond in echo park,
they found eight bodies
at the bottom.
i'll go there, i think,
after he is done.
i'll wrap myself
in blue tarp, be like woolf
with a stone in my pocket
& no one will think twice.
i always had a sadness to me,
after all. now, i am more beautiful.

we are at a circus.
we are not lovers anymore—
this is somewhere in the aftermath
of our loud & bloody affair
& it is raining & there are mice
everywhere, zigzagging across
the carnival cement, panicking
as the water grows around our feet,
ankles, knees. *they're going to drown,*
i keep saying but she doesn't respond,
she wants to know why i'm wearing lipstick.

    who are you always dressing up for?

    they're going to drown.

    who are you always dressing up for?

    they're going to drown.

i once heard the word *conversation*
described as a *progression of exchanges*
but there is no progress here
so maybe i will instead compare this
to the bullet drop—the idea that if you shoot
a gun & drop a bullet from the same location
they will hit the floor at the same time,
hundreds of feet apart.

we are born from the same city
of worry & doubt & fear of loss

but always end up so far
from each other.

she takes me to see the elephants
& i notice that all of the animals
have feeding tubes, bags collecting
pus at the base of their stomachs,
& i keep using the word *inhumane*.

she wants to take a photo
of the fat, gray beast who is dancing
on its doughy hind legs
for a crowd of leering tourists
but when i give her my phone
she digs through it, finds the evidence
of my new, bright life,
my new, bright lover.

     who is she?

     this is inhumane.

     who is she?

     this is inhumane.

we met up to exchange something
of hers i had—an artifact from a time
we thought each other's homes
safe enough to leave our things—
but whatever it was is not here

anymore, the boil of her backbite
is the only thing we hold together
now & so i tell her it's time for me
to go & she agrees, she wants
to stay anyway, she wants to see
the grand finale, the elephant
painting a picture with its nose,
& so i leave her there amongst
the sticky chaos, the sweet wound.
it is still pouring, i am still
heavy with the weight of living,
there is a line of sunburnt
people snaking towards the entrance
& still, no one cares about the mice.

MY MOTHER'S ADDENDUM

every time my mother
tells the story about the time
a man tied her up with zip ties,
she adds something new.
last time it was advice.
when a man holds
a gun to your lower back,
you give him a secret,
you say, "this thing here
is only for us," & he is less
likely to kill you.
today, she adds a reflection.
when it happened,
i wasn't afraid.
it was familiar,
like i had rehearsed it
so many times in my mind
that all i could think was
this is exactly how i imagined it.

with quotes from the Albuquerque Journal*'s coverage of the murder*
of eleven black and brown women, predominately sex workers, and
one fetus found in Albuquerque, New Mexico

We don't believe anyone
is a throwaway
just on the wrong side
of the law
that's the hard part
the wait
there are no answers
only the chase
women that gather dust
and then gone
maybe it was a person
who thought they were doing the Lord's work
murdering prostitutes
addicts and burying them
in a shallow grave
maybe they believed
it was an act of service killing
these girls who
shared a common bond
looked out for each other
in the war zone
soft desert runaways

        [how many bodies
        need to be dug up
before the Albuquerque Police Department
        is comfortable
      with the words *Serial Killer*]

we found two more foot bones
we will continue to search until
we're not finding any more
had we been finding fresh bodies
bodies bodies bodies
bodies bodies bodies
I'd be much more concerned
it's tough work
in missing persons cases
involving women
with criminal lifestyles
they don't want to be found

                    imagine twelve white girls go missing
                       imagine their bodies found
                          before they turn to bone
                       imagine their bodies found
                               how do I write
                              a found poem
                          when there is nothing
                                to be found
                             how can i tell you
                                about a girl
                             who is defined
                             by her absence

                          imagine their bodies

no one cared
whether she ever showed up

[except for those who loved her
who knew she was more than her rap sheet
there are so many more missing
and they're out there somewhere
maybe they are out there
on that mesa
maybe it's time
to take a second look.]

Some things are more a feeling
than they are a memory.
My memory is that I was peering
over something, watching.

*

A man who now I might call a boy,
but back then, a man,
bragged about the bodies
of women he left on the mesa.

*

I have heard men refer to the number of women
they've slept with as their body count.

*

In 2009, out by the volcanoes,
a mass grave, eleven women and one fetus,
found buried in a row like white lines
in a parking lot.

*

Adri taught me that when a man pulls up and asks
if you need a ride you always say yes.
You're always going somewhere
even if you're not.

*

The papers named him
the West Mesa Bone Collector
and named the girls *transient*
and *troubled* and *missing for years*.

*

It was my boyfriend's house.
We never went outside
but I wanted to.
I used to look out the window
and miss my dad.
I used to wake up in pain
and ask him what he did to me
in my sleep.

*

He disposed of the bodies
of sex workers and no one thought
to look until they waned into an outline,
until a dog walker found a girl's femur
in the dirt.

*

We didn't stop getting in cars.
We still needed a ride.
Still needed air-conditioning.
Still thought that saying no
caused more trouble than anything else.

*

He was never caught.

*

One suspect was found stalking
sex workers with a rope and electrical
tape in his front seat.

One suspect strangled a girl to death
and was then shot by her boyfriend.
What is justice when every girl
in the story is either dead or wanted dead?
What is justice when the man didn't do
the *it* we are talking about
but did something like it and buried
her somewhere else?

*

I always thought it was a misnomer—
collector—decorative and terrifying,
but inaccurate. The name
made it sound like a hobby,
like inside his house he
might have a China cabinet
filled with teeth.

[the first call came the day before christmas. i was combing at the green pins of a douglas fir in a holiday tree lot. i wasn't raised with tradition but i lived with a boyfriend now & we were set on playing house the right way. my father says that the babysitter, who now has a name we use instead, came in to the hospital where my mother worked & held out her forearm, pointed to the blackening cyst, the dark bloom of a needle gone awry. my mother dressed it in clean gauze & asked the right questions. she once taught me about motivational interviewing—how, if done properly, a person will tell you all of the things you didn't ask but wanted to know. in this case, it was about the babysitter's father. about her body. about him, awake in her room each night, asking her to keep a secret. about his hand in the hinges of a door, a dog's mouth clamped on his right calf. the ways we cooed at his wounds, named her rage as brief & uniform as a training bra. never asked why his hands gripped a hinge in the first place.]

First rule. Men always want to come inside you so that if they give you a sickness or a baby, you are bound to them forever. People will tell you men don't like commitment and the first rule is that you shouldn't believe them. Remember, sickness or a baby. Neither of which they'll take care of. Men will commit to hurting you but not to healing you. I love commitment and you can believe me on that. Second rule is that you should always believe me because I am always telling the truth. I love commitment because I hate asking questions. I want everything to be big and loud and forever and certain and true. I want to say my mother's whole name. I want you to tell me I have her nose and mean it. I want to be forgiven quickly. I want to say I love you on the first date. I want to play your favorite song until you get sick of it and then never play it again. Tell me you're hungry and I'll fry you an egg. I want to remain young enough to believe I'll never change. I hate epiphanies. I spent my whole life getting into cars with strangers and the worst part was when I recognized them from somewhere I couldn't remember. No, the worst part was when I remembered but couldn't tell if they did too. No, the worst part was when my mouth pulsed around them and they said, *Do I know you from somewhere?* Everyone says I speak in hyperbole but it's just that there are so many ways for things to be the most of what they are. I hate being just a little bit cold in the supermarket. I just want to know where I'm wanted and where I'm not. And that's what I told them, you know? I told them I wanted to make sure the people who hurt me don't ever hurt anyone again. And since you can't ever be sure of that, I took their whole damn bodies.

III.

Big mothership and all. I'll be back, I'll be back.

—AILEEN WUORNOS

but never asked to be the center of attention, just came in, always with a smile on her face, excited to see the people who loved her, which was everyone she ever met, and did i mention she was always happy, never ever ever was she in a bad mood, in fact i don't think anyone ever saw her not smiling, did you? i heard, from a girl at church, that she actually had a smile surgically implanted into her face, i mean just the most bubbly, cheerful girl you've ever met, everyone had a crush on her but no one actually dated her, which made her that much more desirable. she was celibate, i heard, but somehow knew exactly how to make everyone want her, she was like that, such a bright future, so bright we could barely even look at it without permanently damaging our eyesight, she could've done anything she wanted, a nurse, a lawyer, a silent wife, talk about a girl with goals, and on top of all of that? she was a track star, volunteered at the soup kitchen on weekends, and had never disappointed her parents, honestly, come to think of it, there was no one in the world who deserved this less than she did, of all people, i can think of twelve people who deserved this more, it's almost like a sacrifice, maybe the world just didn't deserve her, maybe none of us did, someone so wholesome, so vibrant, so alive, so obedient, so demure, so petite, so tender, so strong, so pretty, so prude, so brave, so quiet, so butchered, so blue. i guess the silver lining is that now the bar isn't so high for the rest of us, we all look better with her dead, just kidding, did you hear she was clutching the fence when they found her? she fought like hell, apparently, it's a shame it was my birthday party and i forgot to invite her, it's a shame no one heard her screaming, the music was just so loud and we were all singing along.

[everything we called hormones. everything we called a temper tantrum. everything i envied. everything i wanted. everything about the babysitter's other life, i wanted, the one i wished so badly to know, the one where she shows me where she hides.]

The men who loved him say,
We never would have expected this,
while his ex-wife goes into hiding.

Before the Visalia Ransacker
turned Original Night Stalker
turned East Area Rapist
turned Golden State Killer was caught—
a former cop, living with his daughter
and granddaughter in a vast and stuccoed
suburban home in Citrus Heights, California—
the detectives were overwhelmed with tips
from women who were convinced
it was their uncle, their boyfriend,
their coworker who once,
in a fit of rage, smashed his computer
screen with an empty mug.

Everyone keeps asking aloud,
Who would have guessed?
Him, of all people.

But we look at each other
across the room.
We roll our eyes.
We have the composite sketch
in our pockets. We held it
up to our fathers
while they slept.

what does it mean
to have an instinct?
does it just mean I was born
to avoid a certain breed of death?

& all of the ways she, i, we, would be unborn
& at the hands of who—men we once loved
or who stumbled upon us, those who we ticked off
or turned down & then, how they will remove
what's left, in small parts or on display
or tucked into bed to be found by the landlord?

even when i am not writing
about the dead girl, i am writing
about the dead girl. even when the girl
in the poem is alive, she is dead
& i am writing about a time when she wasn't.
i am sorry for killing the mood.

it's just that i can't stop thinking about her
& how she must have been afraid like i am,
how she too must have imagined some blue
version of herself. i've always had trouble
getting over people & maybe the dead girl
is the one i never will, the one that got away,
whose favorite song is playing in the pharmacy
while i wait for my medicine.

maybe there is a dead girl inside of me,
inside of all of us, waiting for her turn
to tap dance at the beauty pageant,
maybe right now she's shy & nervous
backstage, but once she hears her name,
she'll shuffle, ball, change
& not blink twice.

[i am sorry to do this to you. i know you've
been hanging on so long. i did not get a
final phone call. i saw her face on the inter-
net and i knew it was a tribute. do you ever
think about which picture they'd use? if
you're reading this, please choose the one
of me in a t-shirt the color of burnt sienna,
my hair in a single braid laid over my
shoulder & across my chest. it is not
my favorite photo but the one where my
mother says i look most like myself. alec
took it. ask him for it. the babysitter died
in the hospital where my mother works.
no, the babysitter died in the bathroom of
my favorite restaurant. then was taken to
the hospital where my mother works &
died again. i hate telling people how it
happened. there is a difference between
fact & truth. the fact is that she overdosed.
the truth is that he killed her.]

ELEGY FOR ALLEGEDLY

In its place, a gap   wide enough for a girl
    to press her finger.
Now a sentence looks   like my teeth.

The boy   touched me in my sleep.
The owner of the cake shop   drove
twenty women to quit their jobs.
What I said   happened is what happened
and not what I remember.

ODE TO THE WOMEN ON LONG ISLAND

after Jennifer Givhan

I want to write a poem for the women on Long Island
who smoke cigarettes in their SUVs with the windows
rolled up before walking into yoga, who hack and curse
in downward dog, and Debra from the next block over, who
has strong opinions about Christmas lights after New Year's,
who says that her body isn't what it used to be
but neither is the economy or the bagels at Rickman's Deli
so who really cares, who, during shavasana, brings up
the rabbi's daughter, who got an abortion last spring,
and Candy in the corner, who is mousy and kind
but makes a show of removing her diamond ring before
class because *it's just too heavy,* calls Debra hateful
and the class takes a sharp inhale through the nose
then out through the mouth. And after class, after Candy
rushes home to check the lasagna, Debra lights up
a smoke and calls her best friend Tammy.

> *So then the girl calls me hateful,*
>
> *hateful, can you believe it? What a word.*
>
> *Some kind of dictionary bitch over here*
>
> *and so you know what I says? I says*
>
> *you don't know the first thing about hateful,*
>
> *wanna know what's hateful? Menopause.*

And it doesn't really matter if Debra actually said that
to Candy (which she didn't) because Tammy is so
caught up that Candy called Debra hateful (which she did)
that next week when Tammy runs into Candy while
shopping in Rockville Centre and Candy asks Tammy
how she's doing, Tammy will adjust the purse strap
on her shoulder and say, *We all have a little coal
in our stocking, Candy,* and Candy will shuffle away,
certain that Tammy knows something about her marriage
that she shouldn't, and she doesn't, she just loves
Debra, who just has a lot of opinions and had Candy given
her the chance to finish her sentence, Debra would have
talked about the reproductive rights march she went to
in the '60s and the counterproductive sex-shaming
methods of organized religion. I want to write a poem
for the women on Long Island, whose words stretch
and curl like bubblegum around the forefinger, who
ask if I have a boyfriend and before I answer, say,

       Don't do it. Don't ever do it. You know

       my friend Linda, she's a lesbian,

       like a real lesbian, and whenever I go

       over there, she lives on Corona over by

       Merrick, by the laundromat, you know where

       I'm talking about? Whenever I go over there

and see her and her wife, what's her name?

I can never remember the girl's name,

anyway whenever I go there I says you know

what I need? I says, a girlfriend, that's what I need.

The women on Long Island smoke weed once a month
on the side of the house after their husbands—Richard Larry
Gary Mike or Tony—go to bed, they let their teenage
daughters throw parties in the basement while they watch
the home network upstairs and keep a bat by the couch
in case anyone gets Mickeyed, even if it's their own sons
who did the drugging, the women on Long Island won't
put it past any man to be guilty, even their kin, who,
after all, have their husband's hands and blood and
last week, when a girl was murdered while jogging
in Queens, the women on Long Island were unstartled
and furious, they did not call to warn daughters.
They called their sons. Took their car keys, their coats,
locked the door, and sat them at the kitchen table.

If you ever, and I mean ever, so much as

make a woman feel uncomfortable

I will take you to the deli and put your

hand in the meat slicer, you think I won't?

You hear me? I will make a hero out of you.

With mayonnaise and tomatoes and dill and onions.

I want to write a poem for the women on Long Island
who, when I show them the knife I carry in my purse,
tell me it's not big enough, who are waitresses
and realtors and massage therapists and social workers
and housewives and nannies and tell me they wish
they would have been artists but

> *life comes fast. One minute you're taking typing classes*
>
> *for your new secretary job in the World Trade Center*
>
> *and the next it's all almost over, life I mean, but I kicked*
>
> *and screamed my way through it, and so will you,*
>
> *I can tell by the way you walk. One more thing:*
>
> *When they call you a bitch, say thank you. Say thank you,*
> *very much.*

Dee & I are rolling silverware in the '50s-themed diner
where we work & "My Girl" is playing on the jukebox for
the forty-second time today. We are still singing along,
even though we don't want to, it's just so easy to say it, *My
Girl,* & Dee stops to tell me she's been on television once,
Dateline, she says *& if there is one thing I know about* Dateline
*it's that you're either on it as a dead girl or as someone who knew
her,* but Dee is neither. Dee is just a woman who stopped
her car one day when she saw a girl, naked, running down
Central with shoelaces tied around her neck & asked if she
needed help. *They've gotta learn that this stuff happens,
somehow,* she says of her daughters, who were piled into
the back seat when it happened, as if defending herself
from some judgment she thought I might make about her
motherhood, but if there's one thing I know for sure it's
that Dee knows how to raise a kid. *She'd been kidnapped,
just picked up right outside of her studio apartment & escaped after
three days of being tortured,* Dee says without a shift in tone,
she never shifts in tone, even when she is explaining to the
group of Harley riders at table 10 that she can't serve them
any more beers, even when she tells off some lady's kid for
wasting the ketchup, even when she hits the high note on
My Girl, somehow, the gavel of Dee's mouth always thuds
the same way. One might even think she is telling me a
story about her daughter's new boyfriend, how he refuses
to wash his dishes, a nuisance, this man who took the girl
& tied her to a bedpost in his Albuquerque apartment.
When they caught him, he led them to a body up north
where the family of the first girl he murdered found her
bracelet in the mud. Dee says, *You can watch the episode,
somewhere.* Three years later, after I've quit the diner, I
move to New York with a man who loves me & I am

drinking a beer in a bar with flat-screen TVs above the liquor shelf that are usually reserved for football but today, they've turned the channel to *Dateline* & there is Dee's face, explaining that she watched the girl for a while as she ran into businesses and was kicked out every time. *No one helped her,* Dee says to the camera. *But my tire iron is under the front seat of my car. I'm not going to let anybody hurt us.*

AILEEN WUORNOS CONVINCES ME TO
PUT DOWN MY DOG

If it was socially acceptable to bite people, every person in this city would have a chunk ripped out of their thigh in the shape of my mouth. I undid a few men and now the state is gonna undo me. When I was a kid, we would scoop out snails from their shells with a spoon and let them sizzle on the sidewalk. How many men do you know who did that to a woman and still get to walk free at the grocery store, try all the samples, go golfing on the weekends in their peach pressed pants? In an article about me, I read that you always know the killer was a woman if the body is left covered with a blanket. Just say it, you always know the killer was a woman if she cleaned up after. Just say it, you always know the killer was a woman if she tried to protect the kid who would discover the body. Even the television shows have titles that show we only do it when we lose it: *Snapped, Enough, Women Who Kill*. But listen, and I'm only telling you this because you asked me, it's better to let her go than shut her inside your house until she's so old you have to carry her up the stairs. She deserves to be somewhere where no one is afraid of her and maybe that place is death. I just think it's funny how, before they kill you, they give you anything you want to eat. Like, don't do me any favors. I'm gonna ask for black coffee because these motherfuckers don't deserve to watch me enjoy something. But you? You boil that dog a whole chicken. You let her rip it to shreds.

you pink armor, lipstick rebel,
steel-cheeked, slit-mouth,
head-to-the-ground, mean girl.

you headphones in but no music
you house key turned blade
you quickstep between streetlights
strainer of pricks and chest-beaters,
laughter is a foreign language
to your dry-ice tongue.

resting bitch face, they call you
but there is nothing restful about you, no,
lips like a flatlined heartbeat,
panic at the sight of you,
scream for their mothers, throat full
of bees, head spun three-sixty
exorcist bitch just trying to buy a soda
just trying to do the laundry
just trying to dance at the party
then someone asks you to smile
and the blood begins to riot
smile, and you chisel away at your own jaw
smile, and you unleash the swarm
into the mouth of a man
who wants to swallow you whole.

one theory is that you were born like this
but i don't believe it. you came out screaming
and alive and look at you now, look at how
you've learned to hide your teeth.

what's wrong with your face, bitch,
your face, bitch, what's wrong with it?

bitch face, i don't blame you for taking
the iron pipe from their hands and branding yourself
with it, for making a flag out of your body bag.

another theory is that you put it on every morning
screw it tight like a jar of jelly
but i don't believe that either.
you woke up like this and have been for years,
how can you sleep pretty
when there are four locks on the door
and the fire escape feels like break-in bait?

they will tell you home is safe zone
no, bitch face is safe zone,
bitch face is home
bitch face is cutting off the ladder
willing to burn in the apartment
if it means he can't get in.

Aileen, do you know how
hard it is to pull a raw blade
from the grip of a Venus razor?
Of course you do. I am always
telling you things you know.

Aileen, every time my father
buys antifreeze he parades it
through the house shouting,
This is poison. Not blue Kool-Aid!
Mostly it's a family joke
but if he didn't do it, I swear one of us
would be cold and foaming
at the mouth by now.

Aileen, stop cutting your bangs.
Aileen, let's go swimming.
Aileen, don't clean your pussy
with anything but water
and even then, don't clean inside.

Aileen, I don't love you. I like you.
Aileen, if you worked for me
I would have fired you already.
Aileen, if you were my neighbor
I would have built an eight-foot-high fence
between our houses.

Aileen, if you were my lover,
I would have to move
out of the country;
I would have to change my name.

Aileen, why didn't you change your name?
Why didn't you run farther?

Aileen, I have no friends left
from high school, tell me what I'm doing
wrong. Tell me why I love to quit.
Tell me why I'm so religious
about absolutely nothing?

Aileen, I'm going to tell you a secret.
Once, back home, I found a duffel bag
full of jewelry and syringes
and metal spoons and a tiny bit of cash.
Was it yours? Did I find you before I found you?

I want to take you home. I think you would like it.
So much land that if you shoot a bullet
it won't hit anything until it skids through the dirt.
So much land that if you scream
it won't hit anything, just break away like mist
a few feet from your mouth.

Aileen, I wish I could've taken you there.
It's too late now. I wish you hadn't hurt all those people.
I'm sorry, I'm sorry, I know you hate it when I say that,
what I meant was that I wish all those people hadn't hurt you.

Aileen, next time you catch me
biting my nails, slap my hand
until it's pink and hot. Aileen, you drink too much.
It makes you violent. Aileen, are we friends?
When did you know? What happens when you go away?

Aileen, I want to be the kind of girl
who writes letters but I find it too time-consuming.
I want to be the kind of girl who does yoga
but I think it's boring. Sometimes I can't listen
to music because it makes me moody.

I am afraid of being impulsive;
whenever I stand on the subway platform
I face the wall, I am not afraid of being pushed,
I am afraid of jumping by accident,
I am afraid it would be easy to believe
I did it on purpose. I didn't want to become
the kind of woman who is always nervous
but I didn't want to become my mother either.

Every hobby I have I picked up from a man
who I wanted to love me. I don't know how
to not become the people I bring home.
I've never been in a fist fight
but I think I'm a great candidate.

You're right, you're right, let me tell you
about the things I love. I love the smell
of October in New Mexico. I love watching ballerinas
beat their pointe shoes against the floor.
I love Melissa's eyelashes. I love
when there's an outlet next to my chair.
I love my father's pillow.
I love the cities that everyone loves.
Thank you, Aileen, I needed that.

Aileen, please forgive me. I won't be there
to watch you go. I won't be there to hold your hand.
Give them a good quote. Aileen, what does it feel like
to be born on leap day? Does it feel like you're always
lying? Does it feel like you're always behind?

Aileen, did I ever tell you
that I was supposed to be born on leap day
but my mother got impatient?
If we had the same birthday,
we could have had a joint party.
We could have had a piñata,
we could have done keg stands
and ditched, smoked cigarettes
behind the bouncy castle.
We could have eaten cake with our hands.

Do you know how to have fun at parties
if there's no one to flirt with?
Never mind I'll stop asking questions
to justify my bad habits,
but there is a right answer,
think about it and tell me later
when no one is watching.

A STORY ENDING IN BREAKFAST

after Ross Gay

This morning, before eating the avocado toast
I made you for breakfast, you stood beneath
a shriek of light on the porch & said, *You know*
you love someone when you look the way I do
right now and feel comfortable, pointing
to your dry elbows and unlaced shoes. & because I imagine
you were talking about allowing your body to exist
in its truest form & because you have let me touch
your most honest skin, I want to tell you a story

about the tricks I have done to make my body
disappear. & because I want you to understand,
I will start from before the beginning, when a girl
is told that in order to be loved properly,
she must make a habit out of service. & because
she is a girl who moves her body to the high
school bell ring, ritual is not foreign to her
& so she justifies it, she says, *Some people need coffee,*
he needs this, & I should clarify that *he* is a boy
but at some point in this story *he* will become a man
& many things will change, but the girl's vindication
is not one of them. She says, *I do plenty of things*
once a day, shower, set my alarm, call my father
to tell him I am safe. She says, *What is love*
if not being needed and unzipping your throat,
if not letting the rats underneath the sink live
because it is the middle of winter?

& though the girl does believe she knows most things,
she is willing to accept a new vocabulary from the boy.

For instance, when he says *now,* he means *here,*
& sometimes *here* is his bedroom floor,
sometimes it is a gas station parking lot,
the dumpsters behind her school. & soon the rush
of being desired begins to harden & the girl must sculpt
a new, doughy mantra to pass the time.
She thinks, *It takes three weeks to form a habit,*
which means twenty-one days until it is as simple
as brushing teeth. & she does, of course she does,
but soon his body becomes immune to the gift
& she begins to realize she cannot bind her mouth
into something tighter, though she dreams of it,

her lips cinched like a velvet pouch.
But because this is merely a dream,
his needs mutate into a tumor with a face
& teeth & hands & soon, she is swallowing
his pillow, tending to the rug burn on her palms
& knees with oil & cloth. She begins to imagine
her body being that of the girl in the magician's box,
whose upper torso rolls away from her hips with ease.
& this is effective until the bell rings & the need becomes
immunity becomes tumor & now he wants it twice,
four times, in the middle of the night but she is asleep
but he wants it so she wakes up

until she learns to not wake up,
learns to lock herself inside of her dreams
& stay there until the sore morning. & by now
the boy has grown a beard & signed a lease
& the girl is preparing to graduate

but all she can think about is running
into an open field of wheat. & it is not long
after this moment that the boy
goes to work & the girl leaves,
not by her own will necessarily,
but by the will of the open door,

& does not return. She says she is triumphant
but covers herself in wool even in summer
& turns to cold steel when a hand is placed
upon her shoulder. & she does not give
the boy's touch a name until he comes to her
in a dream years later & yanks her from sleep
as he always did. & now, the girl is a woman
who can be touched the wrong way but that fact
is merely a footnote in the legend of her life.
Her middle name is not *rip* or *swell* it is Rose,
actually, just like mine, & she still moves to ritual
but now, that ritual shows itself in the grocery store,
where she ponders too long over the ripeness of fruit,
until she finds the perfect avocado, the same one
you found on the counter, ready to be cut open
& pitted & smashed onto bread.

BLOWJOB ELEGY

I didn't know when it happened
that it would be the final time
I pulled my neck back
from beneath his belly.
I don't know whose belly it was
or where he sat or if he trembled
and ached a good ache
towards the sky. What matters
is that there was
a final time—a last swig,
heavy curtains swept across
my lips, intestines working
the closing shift to knead and push
the spore through the center of myself.
Curse the gag and spit.
Curse the barter and fill.
Curse the coming where I plead.
Once I learned how, I held it
in my palm like a slick and heavy coin,
haggled over my sex, hummed to my knees,
raw and wet on the bathroom floor.
It is not for the feeble gut to hold a shaft
against your gums and swallow it.
So praise my iron cheeks,
my fake bitch grin and moan,
praise the day I ditched the parade
of wrap and suck, then cut out my old tongue
and left it to rot in the sun.

the story goes that my brother,
in the first weeks of his life,
was so full of mucus that my parents
were afraid he might suffocate
in his sleep. even his mouth was
bubbling over, green leaking thick
as molasses down his chin.
too far from a hospital
and no healthcare to pay for it,
my father pressed his open mouth
to my brother's nose,
my mother ran to get a bucket,
and he began sucking the phlegm from
his face, hawking it into
the basin until his fat, gurgling baby
let out a clean scream.
i was always jealous of him, my brother,
for the ways my father stopped
him from dying. in every memory
i have he is a hero.
even memories not my own.
when he was selected
for jury duty, the judge asked
if anyone had experience
being assaulted in their home.
so i was removed, my father said
after explaining that he raised
his hand, told the court
about the time my brother pinned him
to the wall and held a shard of glass
against his throat. i think i remember
it happening, i think i must have been there,

i think i was watching from beneath the table,
i think i screamed or did nothing.
my first memory: i stepped on glass
and when i started to cry, my father
laughed and told me to take it out myself.
but maybe that's not true. maybe he took my heel
and put it in his mouth.

a memory is a story
told so well, it becomes
part of the body.

SONNET FOR THE CLOVE OF GARLIC INSIDE ME

Yesterday I groveled in the bathroom,
broke a nail against my denim crotch,
squirmed in line, twisted knees at the grocery store,
dug up a buck to buy a bulb of you,
come evening you were in my bathroom, then
skinned knuckle caught in the quarter machine
plucked, peeled, and wedged into my copper mine
you small burn, you small baker, kneading bread
in a dark, damp room, working overtime.
Sam says, *The taste will make its way to your mouth*
by morning, and that's how you know it worked,
and when I fish you out with my whole hand
you take the thick poison with you, martyr
lily, saint of soil, sear me clean again.

My favorite color is Pepto-Bismol. My favorite color is amoxi-cillin. My favorite color is the calamine bottle. I want to be sick just to swallow you. Offer up my most blood-filled parts and rub pink on the itchy, pink bites. Everyone keeps talking about their muses and I want one too but I don't believe in people, so I nominate you—always using your best baby voice to get the discount but slurring your words the whole time. Something I learned in middle school, after Elise smashed Vivian's head into the sidewalk twice so she got two bumps like horns and every-one called her Devil, is that you never *know* someone is a fake bitch, you can just *feel* it, and that's reason enough to hate them. But I like you for it. I liked Vivian too, to be honest. I like the way you bait and switch. Ponzi scheme doing a pirouette. Boiler room boutique. Tulle, if rubbed hard enough against the skin, starts to feel like sandpaper, the way all of our wounds begin with you. I'm not looking for empowerment. I don't care about femininity, or whatever. I just like the things they call you when you change—coral, bubblegum, millennial, hot. I like the way everyone has an opinion and all you have is a comeback—how you show up to the party with a new haircut and everyone convinces themselves they've never met you, of-fers to pour you a drink, wants to try on your fabulous coat. I fall for the marketing. I bought the mace for girls. The toolbox. If I could make it so, I would make it so: my whole house coated in a layer of you. If my roommate wasn't a goth, we'd have a couch the color of flamingo, fridge like a dipped and dyed Eas-ter egg. Inside, only rosé and sliced grapefruit. Himalayan salt in the cabinet. Beet juice smeared across the counter. My dainty assassin, high-stakes rare steak, wisest rookie on the team, if the thing I hate is the color of you, I love it. There's a pink switch-blade on my counter. If a man holds it to my throat one day, I'll make an exception. For you. I'll smile and say, *Do it*.

ODE TO MY LOVER'S LEFT HAND

There comes a moment on the first night,
after the first of everything, that you admit
the unremarkable talent of your right hand,

and what you don't know is that in this moment
every constellation evolves into a different picture.

Orion's Belt moves its bookend parts to the base, pushes
the middle star to the top to form a triangle.

What I'm saying is, if this right hand is not your best bet
then nothing is what it claims to be, suddenly everything

that calls itself ordinary must be a miracle, the romance
novels at Walgreens must be a Bible, cafeteria food

prepared by the finest chefs, your apartment is Boston's
most coveted museum.

But this is not an ode to your right hand, the one
you call unnatural yet somehow knows how to move

like a cartographer over the map of me,
this is an ode to the moment you climb

to the other side of the bed, pull up the sleeve
of your left arm. What is the word for something becoming

more than whole? What is the word for a bird,
already stunning in its sitting form,

then opening its wings
and the watcher loses their breath?

Is it *Yesterday was the best day but today is forever*?
Is it believing wholly in your breath, until you reach sea level

and learn how easy breath can be? Is the word just *shine*?
Is it *bloom*? What is more beautiful than a hand

alive, nimble, and reaching? Ode to my lover's left hand
is an ode to her voice in the shower,

an ode to the unlocking of our thought-to-be-open throats.
When you make the switch, you begin to tell me about being

ambidextrous, all of the things you can do with both limbs:
texting, basketball, cutting open an avocado for lunch.

But this, you say, *this is for my left hand and my left hand
only.* And then, of course, before I can praise the right

for its already perfect form you *shine,* or *bloom,* or become
the bird in flight and I lose my breath, drop my binoculars,

don't care that I can't see you anymore, because what is sight
really? Your hand unseeable, yes, but inside me also

and what is that if not sight? What is the sky if not my body,
a home for your open and boastful wing.

I AM ALWAYS TRYING TO MAKE
MY POEMS TIMELESS

I'm always talking
around technology
like I get all of my information
from the dusty stacks
at the university library.

Like I know the man's last meal
by heart. Like mentioning an iPhone
makes me a bimbo or something.

What I'm trying to say
is that honestly,
I think the stakes in *Clueless*
are higher than they are in *Star Wars*.

I think Cher preserving her Alaïa
red dress while getting robbed
at gunpoint is literally life or death,
while the galactic war is whatever
because it isn't even, like, real.

Honestly, I found the man my mom
had an affair with on Facebook.
I know your ex just graduated from
nursing school. I think I'm prettier
than all of her prettiest photos.

I don't write poems in my journal
because it takes too long.

I'm always like, *I'm gonna delete my Facebook*
but how will I know about the events happening
near me that I'm never gonna go to?

A rogue dream. Me, in a lilac dress
with an open back showing up on your doorstep.
I am holding your favorite Moscato.
I am holding your favorite fruit.
I am holding your hand as you lead me
through the house to the backyard.
No one was expecting me
but everyone is relieved I am here.
I am dressed perfectly for this weather.
I am so glad I chose this outfit.

I know exactly how to dance to this music.
I left my phone on the counter
in my apartment and I haven't
reached for it once. I walked here with no map.
I ate the perfect breakfast for day drinking.
I am better than you. I smell just a little.

When the sky goes dark, I'll shift
to an evening look with only a leather jacket
and a swoop of liquid eyeliner,
like the magazines promise
you are capable of doing.
Everything is so easy. I love my friends.

Let me tell you the truth, for once.
I don't socialize because I'm afraid

I'll disappoint people. I have spent
so many hours talking on the phone.
I still love chat rooms. The only thing I trust
about myself is how good I am with words.
I can make anyone fall in love with me,
as long as they aren't close by.

ODE TO THE UNPAID ELECTRICITY BILL

To my lover's selectively distant brain—how she lets
only the federal letters sit abandoned in the mailbox
but still checks it each day, hoping for something handwritten,

how she curates a care package for me and calls
the post office every day until it is delivered
to my doorstep, how meticulous she is for love

and reckless for everything that is not love, my lover,
who, after the first night I slept in her bed, woke
to an unworthy light switch, a useless outlet,

and apologized profusely, swore it was not a matter
of money, but rather of mind, promised it wasn't
usually like this, *This never happens,*

the electricity company has a grudge against me,
and I sat in the dark, unfazed, while my phone
battery dwindled, computer dimmed to dead,

until I left for work, not yet knowing that this,
this messy girl, would be my great love,
but for now, dear reader, in this story

she is just a new, frantic girl, certain that her quiet
house is the deal breaker, that after work I won't
return, and will instead find a new lover

who uses a credit card or autopay, and no matter
how much I reassure her, I cannot explain
that the smell of her scalp has enough electricity

to power the village of myself, her voice a reading lamp,
her stomach a power strip, each finger a thousand volts.
My love, if I could tell you I would.

Every day before this has been a day without electricity,
a dark house, digging for my wallet and keys—
Who needs light when I have you?

What is light if not your constant hum? Who are they
to tell me what light is, the men in their navy polos
and white trucks, who are they to name the power

of this house? And so, instead of reassurance, I just
come back. And when I do, of course, my lover
is standing in the living room. There she is,

surrounded by forty candles, surrounded by light,
of course, my lover, there she is, in the organic
light, of course, my lover, there she is fumbling

the flame, telling me she tried her best.

they all do, when I scramble into dinner
unforgivably late with too many bags,
rambling about some new lover
& the way they listen better than the last.
say it, you don't believe me this time
because last time i lost six months
mourning our demise, chain-smoking on a rooftop
next to the airport, where every four minutes
a plane would tear its belly across the sky,
until a new love came along, danced with me
in a parking lot & made sure i drank water.
yes, i thought that one would stay until
my birthday, & no, they didn't, yes,
i was alone by winter, practicing some
familiar grief, my old heart's sacrament.
okay okay, another rolled around by spring,
gone by the next fall, of course i know the pattern,
you teach me nothing when you say it
but say it, i'm always either in love
or heartbroken, say it, i should be alone
more often, i'll admit, sometimes
i don't trust the way i worship, okay?
sometimes i forget who's who. i know
i know, how many gods can a girl have?
who will she go home to when she dies?

but for real this time, they gave us a date,
warning that if we don't change our ways—
our plastic fetish, hunks of hot tire, black smoke
thick as cream spilling into a bird's mouth—ways,
something, i'm not sure what, will happen to make us
gone. so i've gone & decided to collect my avocado shells
& egg cracklings into a bin for soil, as if that will somehow
make the world let me love you longer. i'm not so naïve
to believe your reason is the same—that you dry your hands
on your pants & scold me for letting the sink run
while i scrub a pan, or that you'd carry two gallons of milk
in each arm like identical infants before you would ever ask
for a bag, that the oils & wax & soap in glass bottles
are because you don't want us to die alone in the flood
but instead together somewhere with giddy crickets
& old trees, somewhere past 2040 where we drink from jars
& grow our own spinach, but i think love makes us selfish,
so let me admit that last week, over naan & yellow curry,
when you said that soon there will be war & though you don't
believe in them, you'll have to buy a gun,
because all we'll have to protect are the people we love,
i thought maybe you meant it was me safe behind the door,
jugs of clean water propping up the mattress,
while you stand outside in our desert, rifle against
the spot on your chest where my head goes,
glaring into the filthy horizon,
ready.

So she's a Pisces, right? which means she's already in love
with a girl at the other end of the bar top who drinks

whiskey neat and has a mullet
just like hers, only red.

Pisces love to see some version
of themselves in everything.

Pisces only love things that say something
about who they are.

Aileen is here, at this biker bar
in Daytona, Florida, called *The Zodiac*

because she wants to put something
wet and alive in her mouth.

I don't want to talk about the men
who tried to kill Aileen

or how she killed them first,
I don't want to talk about how self-defense

doesn't make you a serial killer,
about how she said if a hundred men

had tried to rape her,
she would have killed a hundred men.

Tonight, I want to talk about two girls kissing against a wall
in an alley behind a lesbian bar. I want to talk about the fact

that there are almost no lesbian bars left in the country
and one theory as to why is that queer women

are more likely to fall in love and move in together
and ultimately stop going to bars.

I was sad once, that there were no bars
for gay girls in my town,

and then I remembered
that love can kill an industry.

If I ever look back and think,
I should have spent more time going out

with my friends, at least I will know
I spent most of my life in love.

I want to talk about how Aileen and Tyria went home
and stopped going to Zodiac. How Zodiac is out of business.

I want to talk about
how they never went on a date,

they simply went home together
and didn't leave the house for a week.

When Tyria suspected Aileen had killed
more than one man, it was because Aileen brought her gifts

that she couldn't have afforded to buy.
I want to talk about how, in the end, Tyria said,

We were more like sisters than lovers.
In the end, Tyria was promised immunity.

In a phone call tapped by police, Aileen called Tyria
her *right arm,* her *left arm,* her *breath,*

how all Tyria could say back was *Please tell them,*
please say it out loud. But Aileen didn't want to talk about it.

She wanted to talk about love. So Tyria would hang up,
unsuccessful, and the officer would tell her to

Say it like this, tell her she'll get off,
tell her it won't be so bad.

But how, each time, for three days straight,
the police listened to Aileen talk about love.

About her right arm. Her left arm.
Her breath. Her breath. Her breath.

[i don't mean to skip over a whole life but if i told you everything we would be here all day. but here is something i can give you that is not meant to serve as a clue or tragedy, just a true story. when *titanic* was released on vhs, it was so long that it came in a box set of two tapes & the babysitter reserved a whole evening for us to watch it. we lay on our stomachs with our heads propped up in our hands, elbows on the floor of her plush-carpet den, & when the sex scene came on, she asked me to get her a glass of water & by the time i came back, rose's hand had already run down the foggy window. when he drew her naked he let me stay. when the ship split in two i asked her if this was a true story & she said yes. when jack froze against the wooden door i asked if this was a true story & she said no. *but if there was no love story,* she said, *it would just be a movie about a bunch of people dying.*]

is that it happened somewhere on the 101
between Portland and Arcata
where Maríajosé and Joaquina,
having remembered what I'd said
about the giant trees, how they remind me
that everything I feel is small and temporary,
would wake me up and point out
the window every time we passed
them, a family of those burgundy beasts
off the highway, some as wide as
our fifteen-passenger van. in the end,
the trees were irrelevant, it was the fact
that someone saw them and thought
of me, shook me awake
and made me look.

ALL OF THE MISSING GIRLS ARE
HANGING OUT WITHOUT US

let this be the folklore. not in a field.
not in a river, not mouth half-open,

knock-kneed under the tall grass
behind the baseball field.

not in a park or at the bottom of a drained pond,
not in their boyfriends' trunks, their boyfriends' closets,

or between the floorboards
in his house. they are alive

but not in a basement, not scanning
a grocery store bulletin board

for a picture of their young and gone face. no, the girls
are having a contest: who can catch the most tineola moths

in a mason jar, who can sprint back to the barnyard
fastest to set it on the kitchen windowsill

during the golden hour, the amber light
and its brief devour.

the only prize is that the winner gets to see it first—
a horde, chestnut-colored and coated in honey,

slapping against the glass walls and tin roof,
unbroken by the human hand.

all of the girls will flock around it—a mob of soft and angry,
a lantern alive, kaleidoscope of wings—

for a moment they are all in the same place,
until dark, when the girls have lost interest

and gone to sleep beneath each other's warm pits and legs,
at which point the oldest girl will carry the jar

out onto the porch and unscrew its lid,
let the gentle bodies spill out like wedding doves,

frantic and blooming into night.

every night, a cup of juniper tea.
a window cracked for breeze.

a drawer of clean knives
in the kitchen. only used for fruit.

never under my pillow. my sleep,
a steady march. it's been so long,

that the thing i read that one time,
about how he woke the girls up

with a flashlight to the face, is rusted
and untouched at the bottom of my skull.

you can find the pink mace in thrift stores,
lipstick turned to blade, nail polish that changes

color when dipped in a drugged drink. a reminder
of the rituals we had to keep each other out.

a girl watches the sky go and keeps laughing.
the water only knows her body

moving. we walk everywhere. there is no such thing
as *hurried* unless to beat the clock. i am old.

my body a thousand lines, feeble and aching
to sit. my hair still sheds at the same rate

but now, the color of oysters, silver
and wet and curled in my drain. my feet

still fat and full of blood in the heat.
i still love to smoke but still don't, i still think

i will pay for the days i did. i still have the memories—
the ways i made this breed of fear a religion. the ways

i rehearsed my day to be taken. but most days,
i choose to forget what it was like

when they walked the Earth—the men
who wanted their say in when a girl's body

goes still, the men obsessed with our necks,
the men who earned nicknames like Zodiac,

BTK, Ripper, Bone Collector, men who
said they would be gone in the dark.

ultimately, it was a sickness that killed them.
a sickness reserved only for the ones

who wanted us gone. the papers want to tell us about
the science of it and i've heard things, how it forms

a host in the part of the brain that houses
violent fantasies. how the worse the thoughts get,

the worse the sickness gets, grows so big,
it pushes out the teeth. i remember seeing them,

heads cocked back at parties and laughing with
their jaws slung open, a quick flash of missing

molars. the worst ones had dentures, posters
warned women to reject date offers from men

with a veneer smile. eventually, it climbs towards
the neck, pushes the blood towards the surface

till the flesh grows blue and bulging. you didn't see
those ones out much, quarantined by their mothers

who shoved romance novels in their faces, begged
them to thirst for something tender. but most often,

it was too late, most often incurable, and soon,
their chests collapsed, quiet as a slow-leaking balloon.

yes, there were vaccines. yes, a surgeon with conviction
in the good spell of his blade. yes, many a man

with his throat cut open, or a small slice behind his ear.
but always, they return. if left alone for long enough,

the blue would crawl back to the stage and sing.
all we have now are the memorials in this blessed

apocalypse. gravestones shaved clean and wordless,
planted by their mothers to mourn in shame.

the radical girls will rip them from the ground
and smash them along the highway, a trail of shattered

stone for miles. all that's left are those of us who remember.
the rest are newborns or missing.

what do you call a feeling
that no longer lives in your body?

do you call it a memory? do you call it an ex?
do you call it and beg it to come back?

sometimes i say it out loud to see if i can still pronounce it.
i say it into the mirror. watch the way my mouth wrestles.

then i snatch it by the neck and squeeze it till it's limp,
shove it back down to the bottom of the river.

ACKNOWLEDGMENTS

Thank you to the editors of the following journals, which first published these poems:

"A Story Ending in Breakfast," "The Lover As a Dream," and "Here Is What You Need to Know"—*Poetry City*, Vol. 8.

"The Scholar" and "The First Shave"—*Tinderbox Poetry Journal*

"Gamble"—*The Missouri Review*

"Backpedal"—*Muzzle* magazine

Thank you to Button Poetry for giving the following poems a home in *New American Best Friend*: "The Scholar," "The First Shave," "Ode to the Women on Long Island," "Backpedal," "Ode to My Bitch Face," "The Summer of 2008 at Altura Park," and "The Autocross."

I owe so much to my agent, Mackenzie Brady Watson, for finding me and then finding this book inside of me. You changed my understanding of myself as a writer and no amount of words can properly express my gratitude for that gift.

Thank you to my editors, Whitney and Clio, for your excitement and joy and for believing in my ability to write the book I wanted to read. Thank you for taking a chance on me.

Thank you Avideh, Maria, Jess, Dhara, and the entire Dial Press and Random House team for your incredible support.

Thank you to my booking agents, Peter Agoston and Luna Olavarría Gallegos, for your persistence and making my dreams come to life.

Thank you to Melissa Lozada-Oliva, for your sisterhood, for coming with me to Vermont, for encouraging me to say more and teaching me what it means to keep friendship alive. To Maríajosé and Joaquina, for saying yes to riding with me through the most important two months of my life. Thank you for being the most gutsy bitches I know. What I know about unconditional love I know because of you. Thank you for healing me.

To the rest of my patient friends, who read many versions of this book and helped it become what it is now: Sam Rush, Hieu Minh Nguyen, Desiree Dallgiacomo, and Sierra DeMulder. Oompa, for the love you gave me during so much of the creation of this book.

Thank you Paul Tran, Rachel Gubow, Blythe Baird, Donte Collins, Alec Loeser, Noah Brown, Edwin Bodney, Angelica Maria Aguilera, Ashlee Haze, Raych Jackson, Jazzy Dena, Mason Granger, Mahogany Browne, Josh Karp, Jeremy Radin, Megan Falley, Andrine Pierresaint, Chrysanthemum Tran, and Janae Johnson for above all else, your friendship. Thank you, Niko, for showing me the stars.

Thank you to my family for continuing to encourage that I tell my story how I remember it. To Ms. Bernstein, without you I would not be a writer. Thank you for seeing something in me that took much longer to see in myself.

Faustino Villa, Khalid Ali, Mickey Figueroa, Eva Crespin, Reed Adair Bobroff, Kenn Rodriguez, Trae Dahl, Hakim Bellamy, Joe Romero, Jessica Helen Lopez, and Damien Flores, thank you for raising me.

To the girls I grew up with and the women and girls I've

lost: Stephanie S., Barbara, Natalie, Taylor C., Taylor H., Jenny, Shauna, Stephanie D.C., Avry, Meg, Joanna, Leigh, Lydia, Gabby, Sam, and DJ.

To my readers and listeners and viewers who have been so endlessly supportive over these surreal few years, my body of work belongs to you. You are my favorite fangirls.

This book is for all of the women who have survived violent men or whose lives were taken by them—who have either become celebrities in the wake of their deaths or who have gone unnamed by the public. I write for you.

ABOUT THE AUTHOR

Olivia Gatwood has received international recognition for her poetry, performances, and work as an educator in sexual assault prevention and recovery. She is the author of the poetry chapbook *New American Best Friend*. Her poems have appeared in such publications as *Muzzle*, *Winter Tangerine*, *Poetry City*, *Tinderbox Poetry Journal*, and *The Missouri Review* and have been featured on the BBC, MTV, and HBO, among others. She is from Albuquerque, New Mexico.

oliviagatwood.com
Facebook.com/oliviagatwoodpoetry
Twitter: @oliviagatwood
Instagram: @oliviagatwood

ABOUT THE TYPE

This book was set in Bembo, a typeface based on an old-style Roman face that was used for Cardinal Pietro Bembo's tract *De Aetna* in 1495. Bembo was cut by Francesco Griffo (1450–1518) in the early sixteenth century for Italian Renaissance printer and publisher Aldus Manutius (1449–1515). The Lanston Monotype Company of Philadelphia brought the well-proportioned letterforms of Bembo to the United States in the 1930s.